Designing a School Play

Designing a School Play

Peter Chilver and Eric Jones

Illustrations by Eric Jones

Taplinger Publishing Company
New York

First published in the United States in 1969 by
TAPLINGER PUBLISHING CO., INC.
New York, New York

Library of Congress Catalog Card Number: 77-86971

ISBN 0-8008-2171-8

Second Printing

Contents

Foreword 9

I Introductory points 11
Seeing it in perspective: the need to experiment 11
There is no *one* way: the theatre is constantly in a state of transition 12
The school itself 12
The stage and the hall 13
Flexible staging 13
Some practical points in flexible staging 15
    Using the apron and main stage 15
    Furniture on apron or open stages 15
    Exits and entrances 16
    Lighting 16
    Seating 16
Theatre in the round 16
The open stage 18

II Planning 20
Personnel 20
The first production conference 21
Drawing up the production schedule 22
Schedule for the final rehearsals 22

III Plan into action 24
The Director: his overall conception of the production 24
The Director and Designer: initial conference 24
The Designer: getting ideas on to paper 25
The Designer: detailed plans 25
Sight lines 29
Presenting the model 30
Wardrobe 30
Programmes, handbills, tickets, publicity 31

IV A basic approach to stage design 33
Basic types of design 33

V Stage lighting 42
General principles 42
The different kinds of stage lighting 44
A basic approach to stage lighting 46
Working out the stage lighting 51
Setting up the lights 54
Operating the lights 55
Lighting the sections of the acting area 54
Front-of-house lights 55

VI Building   56
Flats   56
Stairs   62
Rostra   63
Trucks   65
Profile scenery   65

VII Painting   67
Basic points   67
General points   71

VIII Specific designs   72
Epic Drama   72
Restoration Comedy   75
Victorian Music Hall   77
Macbeth   78
Pride and Prejudice   81
Gaslight   84

Postscript   86

Terms used in staging
and scenic design   87

Index   93

Foreword

This book is intended to be of value to all those who are concerned in any way with the staging of a school play – whether as director, designer, stage manager, lighting director, carpenter or actor. It attempts to place the work of the designer into perspective alongside the work of all those others who are involved in the same end product. It looks at the problems of design from all the basic viewpoints – in terms of the actual staging of the play within the limitations of particular schools and particular school buildings, in terms of the various approaches to scenic design, and in terms of the problems encountered in lighting, building and painting the designs.

The days are rapidly disappearing when a school play is judged simply in terms of whether it is enjoyable to be acting in it, and when the real theatrical impact on the audience is largely ignored. The increasing importance attached to educational drama is fostering a new kind of school play, one in which the value to the performers and the production personnel from working on a dynamic and artistic project is only equalled by the genuine 'theatre' which the project eventually creates. It is this increasing awareness that the school play can really be good theatre and good education also that distinguishes the best work in the schools today. Some schools undoubtedly lag far behind. Others have been pioneering the way for many years, quite unnoticed from outside. It is with those who see the school play in terms of such potential distinction that this book seeks to ally itself. And it is to those – staff and pupils – who wish to know more about the basic technical points involved in design and staging, that the book is planned to be of use: for the whole point of a project is that everyone becomes involved in some way in the work that everybody else puts into it. And in this way the project becomes, over a very wide area of activities, genuinely educational.

I Introductory points

Seeing it in perspective: the need to experiment

There is now, and presumably always will be, a great deal of argument about the merits of one kind of 'theatre' as opposed to another, or about the merits of staging a play in this way rather than that. There are advocates of 'theatre in the round', of 'theatre in the three quarters', of the 'open stage' theatre and of the old 'plush and gilt' theatre. And many of these advocates will argue that only their particular form of staging is the 'right' one, and that all the others are unexciting or inartistic or both. As far as the professional theatre is concerned it is often impossible to demonstrate the merits of any of these arguments, for the simple reason that there are few theatres which are so equipped as to allow experiment with the different forms of staging. But in schools it is perfectly possible for all the different techniques of staging to be experimented with. A lot will of course be determined by the nature of the play or show to be produced. Similarly much will depend on the type of audience for which the show is designed. For instance, a demonstration by the drama society in the art of improvisation, or an illustrated history of drama, may be intended only for a small audience of pupils who are invited to stay behind for an hour or so after school. Such an entertainment may well lend itself much more easily to a simple 'theatre in the round' technique of presentation than would a full-scale musical or revue. But regardless of the nature of the show or play itself, it is both possible and desirable at all times to experiment in the mode of staging and to combine as many different modes as possible. Rather than approach the problems of design and staging with fixed ideas and prejudices, one should ideally see the whole business in flexible terms.

There is no one way: the theatre is constantly in a state of transition

It is always worth remembering that no part of the theatre was ever created whole. In its totality it is made up of many diverse and bastard elements. The theatre is a rag-bag of make-believe. At no time in its history has it been anything but more or less in a state of transition. Men give to it what they can, and take from it what they want. It has come into being as a forum where men collectively exercise the imaginative impulse. In one form or another it has survived many civilisations, and endured longer than many known religions.

Just as there is no aspect of the life of the theatre which has been created whole, so there is no *one* way of doing anything. There is no 'right' procedure as opposed to which all others are 'wrong'. All is experiment of one sort or another. Even if a well-tried formula or method is adopted, then even that is an experiment. What will actually work in any specific production cannot be accurately known in advance, even though the same or similar technique may have worked in other productions.

If, as Director or Designer, you conceive an apparently unconventional approach to a problem, then the uppermost questions in your mind should be – Is it practical? Is it going to work?

The school itself

In the devising of a school play everything in the end depends on, and is governed by, the school itself. And the school comes before the play. This is true in many different ways. First the life of the school, social as well as academic, must not be destroyed by the activities involved in producing the play. Balance must be maintained. This means, among other things, choosing the right time of year to produce the play, and choosing the cast and production personnel from among pupils who can legitimately spare the time involved in rehearsing and presenting the show. It also means tailoring the production, and in particular the scenic designs, to the facilities available in that particular school. Obviously, a large comprehensive school, with well-furnished art and woodwork departments, can produce scenery on a much more lavish scale than can a small secondary or grammar school. But the teacher in a smaller school may well find some comfort from the fact that in the professional theatre the best in quality is not often related to the most lavish scenery and expense.

The personality of the school will also have to be considered. Is there a drama tradition? Do the speech and personalities of the pupils themselves suggest certain types of drama more than others? Does the school play tend to attract a wide selection of adults from the community, or do the audiences consist almost entirely of pupils? Is there a liaison with other schools? If the school is a boys' school, is it possible to establish links with a girls' school?

The stage and the hall

But the most important point for consideration is the stage, and the hall. Few school halls or school stages are designed either primarily or at all with a view to their use for drama productions. The commonest faults are:

Lack of space in the wings or backstage
Limited acting area on the stage itself
Low proscenium arch
High ceiling
Very long hall
Bad acoustics
Too many windows
Too few doors for exits or entrances
Insufficient depth to stage
Stage too high from the ground
Gallery round the hall, from which it is virtually impossible to see the stage
Too much noise from outside traffic
Lack of dressing-room amenities, including lack of adequate space, lighting or washing facilities
Lack of suitable facilities for adequate stage lighting.

Flexible staging

The answer to these problems is to get away as far as possible from the use of the stage itself and to think in terms of flexible staging. By this we mean simply using the stage in combination with some form of apron or fore-stage, or leaving the stage altogether and employing the techniques of the theatre in the round or the theatre in the three quarters, in which case the stage may perhaps be used for seating part of the audience.

You should consider the following possibilities:
(i) The first practical step is to see if the stage can be extended by the addition of an apron stage. An extension of 6 feet may perhaps be enough. Can it be made a permanent structure? Or, if it is to be temporary, is it possible for the technical department to build it? Or can it be hired or borrowed? Or can it be built up with existing rostra?
(ii) Alternatively it may be possible to construct a completely independent apron stage immediately in front of the main stage but at a lower level. This can be of whatever size you wish, and of any shape. It is not necessary to have all the apron at the same level. This form of staging is ideal for epic plays or for any kind of spectacular entertainment where large crowds have to be moved about the stage and where a sense of the vast and the expansive is essential to the dramatic impact of the play. Also, where an apron stage is used in combination with a curtained main stage, then sets can be changed behind the main curtain while the action of the play continues on the apron. But be careful not to design the production in such a way that a major scene has to be played in front of the main curtain, for this will rob the scene of its full dramatic impact. In all major scenes the full stage, with its varying levels, should be in use.

Illustrations 1 and 2 show the simplest forms of stage extension.
(iii) It may be desirable to abandon altogether the use of the main stage and to erect a temporary structure which is an independent open stage. It may be possible to use say, the gymnasium or a covered badminton court, or indeed to set the play in the open air in the playground or sports field. Alternatively the

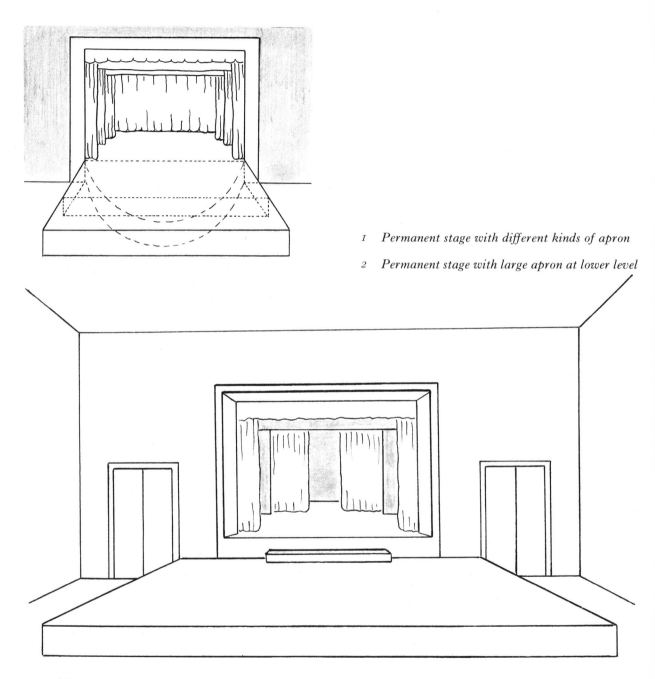

I Permanent stage with different kinds of apron

2 Permanent stage with large apron at lower level

14

hall itself may be the best location. If the hall is square, then you should experiment with setting the stage at an angle in one of the four corners. In any event, remember to keep access to the stage both easy and manageable. If the stage is set in one of the four corners then enough space can be left behind it to create a complete 'backstage' where the props can be laid out, where the prompter (if used at all) can sit, where performers wait before making their entrances and where the sound effects man can work. With an 'escape' door to the dressing-rooms, this set-up can be ideal.

If the stage is set in the open air, then a tent can be erected immediately behind the stage.

Some practical points in flexible staging

Space. This should be the basis of all your thinking:

Space on stage
At the sides of the stage
Behind stage
In the dressing-rooms
In the audience
For easy access by the audience to the hall
For the electrical department (whether backstage or out-front)
For the sound effects man
For the performers to get on and off the stage.

These various spaces do not necessarily have to be large, but they must all be thought about, and each person/department must have *some* space that is genuinely adequate for their particular activity.

Using the apron and main stages

Remember that if a large independent apron stage is being used then the audience will be that much farther away from the main stage. Therefore you should avoid using the main stage too exclusively: let the action spill over as much as possible from the main stage on to the apron, and vice versa. Remember too that many school stages are far too high for the audience to see clearly what is happening on the upstage area, and that in such cases the best acting areas are downstage of the main stage and the whole of the apron stage. Alternatively you may find that while the apron stage is useful, it is too low to sustain much of the action: in such a case it may be possible to break up the apron into various levels. The apron will be too low for instance, where people seated at the back of the hall are unable to see any character on the apron stage in full length. Since it is not always possible to raise up the levels of the audience, this position may be unavoidable, as it may be essential for other purposes to have at least part of the apron at the low level. The only answer is once again to keep the action moving between the level of the apron on to the main stage.

Furniture on apron or open stages

If the production calls for the setting of furniture on an apron or open stage, then you should use as little as possible, and it should be as low as possible. If the furniture has to be placed or removed during the action of the play, then this should be incorporated wherever possible into the action of the play: let the actors do the necessary operations as part of the play. Avoid doing such jobs during blackouts – or if it is absolutely essential to use the blackout, then at least be sure to rehearse this, *in a blackout,* several times, in order to see whether it is in fact possible.

Exits and entrances

An apron stage is, of course, of limited use unless it is possible to get on and off the apron without using the main stage. In some halls you can create temporary wings at the side of the apron by using screens or curtains or by building some kind of temporary arch or doorway. In any event, it is also a good idea to use in addition, entrances and exits through the audience. This means that gangways must be reasonably wide, not only because of fire regulations, but also because people sitting at the end of a row of seats often like to stretch their legs. Keep in mind also the need to have someone controlling the doors during the entire performance to ensure that doors are opened at exactly the right moment for the actors, and that they are closed properly after they have entered.

Lighting

With any form of apron or open staging, it is important to make sure that the lighting used for the illumination of the acting area does not also in any direct way light up the audience. This is something that can only be worked out by trial and error, and this means leaving plenty of time to experiment. Those sitting nearest to the stage are bound to be caught by a certain amount of 'throwback' illumination: this is unavoidable.

If a performance is being given in daylight, whether indoors or out of doors, gauge where the strongest light will be coming from, and be sure to seat the audience with their backs to it.

Seating

Seating for the independent open stage can be just as flexible as you wish. Avoid having the front row of the audience too near the stage. Otherwise the audience may find themselves too much illuminated by the throwback from the stage lighting. Also, if the stage is built up by rostra and is quite high, it can be unnerving, for both the actors and the audience, to find the players almost standing in the laps of the people in the front row.

Do *not* have a central gangway, for this takes away an entire block of the best seats in the house.

Have gangways on either side of the rows of seats.

Give as much space as possible between one row and the next.

Do not place seats directly behind each other. Stagger the seating.

Wherever possible, try to elevate at least some of the seating.

Theatre in the round

Let us now consider the complete 'theatre in the round'. By this term we mean any staging where the audience completely surround the acting area, whether it be round, oval, rectangular or square. The actual shape will be conditioned by the needs of the time. Points to keep in mind are:

Generally speaking, theatre in the round should be fairly intimate, with the stage or acting area at ground level.

There should be at least two entrances.

The audience seating should be elevated in such a way that each row is at least 1 foot higher than the row in front. Three or four rows all round are usually enough. This tends to mean that 'intimate' shows are better suited to this kind of staging, but it is by no means impossible to mount large-scale epics and spectaculars on such stages: these will involve the use of a larger acting area broken up into various levels.

Remember that since the audience will be looking down on to the floor of the stage, the design and/or the covering of the floor will be of paramount importance. It can, for example, be a black and white patio, suggesting a classical formality, or it may be richly carpeted to suggest a Victorian atmosphere, or it may be so coloured as to suggest a particular mood.

Furniture must be kept to a minimum, and nothing taller than an ordinary table should be employed.

Whatever the size of the acting area, the audience must be allowed to see and hear everything that is going on – and what is more important, they must actually *feel* that they see and hear, even when various performers are standing with their backs to them. Always remember that there is no *one* focal point on an arena stage and there is no 'best' position.

If the acting area is quite a large one, and some rostra or platforms are used, then be sure to leave a fairly wide space at ground level all round the rostra.

Costumes and props assume tremendous significance, and they more than anything else will help to establish the period and the atmosphere. They must be first rate, especially as they will have to stand up to much closer inspection than they would have to on a conventional proscenium stage setting.

Lighting will have to be all round the stage and will need to be set high with, at the minimum, twelve baby spots.

Theatre in the round can be a very exciting experiment, and while it is a pity to be deterred by the various problems, it is essential to face them fully. Keep in mind that it is a medium of which both actors and audiences have the least experience. For the Director too, it poses great problems in moving the actors. Whereas on the conventional proscenium stage one usually moves actors on their own lines, on the arena stage it is permissible and often essential to move actors around on other people's lines, thereby giving the audience on all sides a chance to see the action 'in the round'. All this movement has to be thought out very carefully, otherwise the whole production becomes messy and confused. The Director must be constantly on the move throughout the rehearsals in order to see the many different points of view from which the audience will see the play. He must also keep the action moving in such a way that it is neither a game of statues nor a kind of shambling fun-fair. And for the actors there is the additional responsibility of having to project in many different directions at the same time.

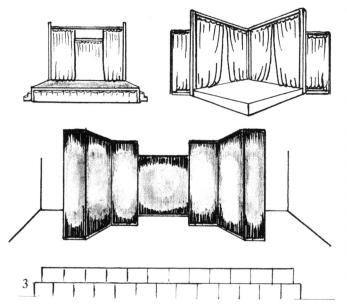

The open stage

Perhaps the kind of open stage that lends itself most readily to initial exploration and experiment is what we may call the 'angled' open stage. This is an open stage set up at one corner of the hall with the audience seated round it in a fan shape which can increase in width as it recedes. This creates quite a large seating capacity, but also gives all the audience a good view of the stage. The front of the stage does not have to be straight: it can jut out into the hall like the corner of a box, or it can be completely irregular. Illustrations 3, 4 and 5 give examples of simple 'independent' stages. Illustration 6 suggests one basic kind of angled open stage.

3, 4, 5 Different examples of independent stages

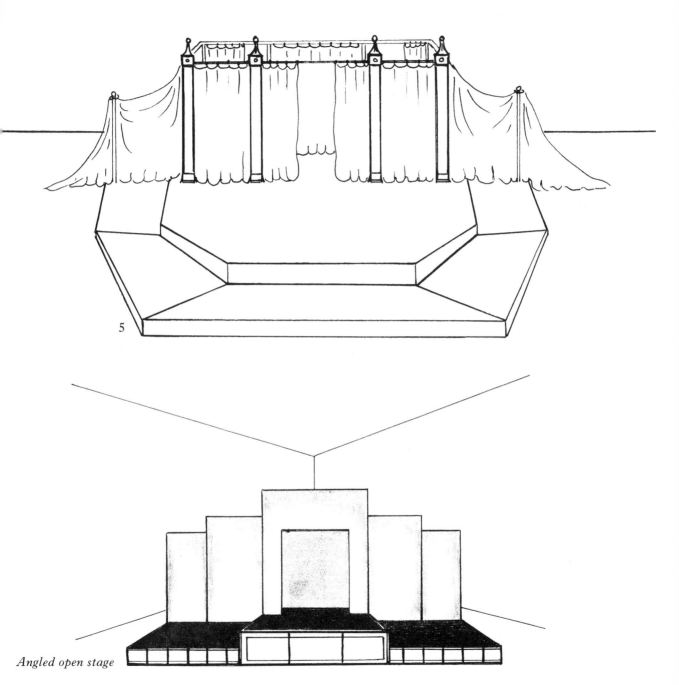

5

Angled open stage

19

II Planning

Personnel

The people and departments involved will be:
The *Director* and his *assistant*.
The *Designer* and his *assistant*.
The *Production Manager* – supervises arrangements for rehearsals, draws up rehearsal schedules, arranges all business matters such as printing programmes/tickets, hiring of costumes, and publicity, and is responsible for the general well-being and discipline of the whole venture.

The *Stage Manager* or *Stage Director* who runs the show at performances, and works on the show from the very first rehearsals, keeping an up-to-date copy of the script which is clearly marked with all the actors' moves and all other instructions, including relevant notes on props, lighting and sound effects.
The *Stage Manager's assistants*. The Stage Manager will need at least three assistants, one of whom will be responsible for props.

A *Sound and Effects Technician* to work the panatrope or tape recorder and to assume any relevant duties.
A *Carpenter* and *technical construction team*.
The *Lighting Designer* or *Lighting Director*.
The *Chief Electrician* who may also be the Lighting Designer, but in any event it is essential to have at least one fully capable and reliable electrician on any production.
Three *Assistant Electricians* – more if necessary.
Wardrobe Master or *Mistress*.
At least two *Wardrobe Assistants* who can if necessary act as dressers during the actual performances.
Musical Director (if a musical show) and his assistant.
Front-of-House Manager who will also usually manage the box office. He will need at least three assistants.
Refreshments or *Catering Manager*.
The *Actors*.

If you take into account the number of people likely to be involved in building and painting scenery, you can see that in a major production it is perfectly possible for anything between sixty and a hundred people to be involved. It is therefore perhaps worth suggesting that you do not plunge into so vast an enterprise for your first venture as a Director. Begin with a relatively simple production which does not involve quite such elaborate technical preparation – such as an evening of improvisations or a music hall.

It is worth stressing at this point that the school play is a project – one of the most exciting and rewarding of all the various projects that a pupil may encounter. But any project loses its educational value if it is poorly organised, or if the real 'behind the scenes' operations are carried out by the staff and without reference to or consultation with the pupils. The pupils themselves, including the members of the 'acting' company, should perform most of the jobs listed above. In exceptional instances they may perform all of them. The Stage Manager, for instance, should very definitely be a pupil, and so should the Production Manager. This does not mean that the teaching staff should disappear altogether – part of the value of the project is the excellent opportunity it offers to young people to apprentice themselves to teachers who are skilled in various aspects of theatre. But it does mean that, where, say, the Director and Designer are teachers, then they should have pupils working closely with them as their assistants. The following year perhaps the pupil will assume the role previously performed by the teacher.

Furthermore, the pupils should be actively involved in all the various preparations for the production, right from the very start. In this way they learn a great deal about organisation in general, quite apart from what they learn about the theatre itself.

Presenting a school play is a project of almost unique complexity. Departments, pupils and teachers have to work together over a period of time and with a degree of concentration which can become harassing if not properly organised. Furthermore, it all has to be done within the framework of the normal day-to-day functioning of a school where the routine of work cannot be ignored or upset. Among other things, this means that every one involved has to sacrifice quite a bit of his free time. This is another good reason why time must not be wasted. It also means that for the Director and the Designer, as well as for everyone else, it is necessary to have a good practical knowledge of human nature, and a quiet wisdom and patience which are little short of the divine.

The first production conference

Once the personnel have been recruited and the Director has broadly thought out his plan of campaign, the first step is for the Director to hold a conference for all the members of the production team. The agenda at this conference will include the following:

Statement by the Director of his overall conception of the show and of the way it is to be done;

Statement as to when rehearsals are to start and when the production is to be staged;

Statement as to when the next production conference is to be held. By the time of this second meeting the Designer should have worked out his ideas for designing and staging the show. Hence the date of this second meeting will depend on how long it is likely to take the Designer to work out his ideas and confirm them with the Director;

General discussion of the work of each department, including possible dates for any relevant business, such as releasing publicity or sale of tickets;

General discussion of all and any aspects of the production.

By the time of the second conference, the Production Manager, in close consultation with the Director and the Designer, should have drawn up a complete *schedule* of the production.

Drawing up the production schedule

After the general shape of the designs has been agreed upon by the Director and the Designer, the next step is a rough breaking down of the work involved for each department, and of the time during which the work has to be done.

It is always important for the planner of the production to allow time for error, miscalculation and re-thinking. If, for instance, the Wardrobe Mistress says that she needs three weeks to make say a dozen costumes, then, as a matter of practical common sense, a further week should be allowed for this on the actual schedule.

Time must also be allowed for every one to experiment and generally to adopt an empirical approach to the work. Just as a good director of actors always allows the actors to experiment and improvise, so a good director of operations allows all the personnel sufficient freedom to expand and to play around with varying ideas.

It is worth noting also, that while perfectionism is admirable unto itself there is little value in a perfectionism which serves only to discourage others. If the Director, for instance, considers any set automatically worthless unless it is up to the standards of those now employed by the Royal Ballet, then he is pursuing a line of reasoning that is not only unrealistic but which would also have been dangerous in the formative days of the Royal Ballet itself.

A few points about the schedule:

It will list all the activities of each department, plus dates for the completion of each activity;

It should be circulated among all the personnel. Every one should know what is expected of himself and of others;

The production schedule can only be drawn up *after* the rehearsal schedule has been drawn up, for otherwise the Director cannot be sure that the actors will be ready by the time the show, technically, is ready. But it is often a good idea to draw up only the first month or so of the rehearsal schedule in any detail, and to wait until a few weeks of actual rehearsals have elapsed before attempting to draw up the remainder.

Schedule for the final rehearsals

The allocation of time for the final weeks of rehearsal is always a fairly complicated matter. The following should be provided for:

(i) Complete runthroughs of the play, starting

at least a fortnight before the first performance – but without sets or costumes.

(ii) In the case of musical shows, specific music rehearsals.

(iii) A costume parade at least three days prior to the first performance.

(iv) Specific times set aside for the setting up of scenery and the final painting of it and 'touching up'.

(v) Time allocated for setting up the lights and plotting their positions, and for rehearsing the lighting cues.

(vi) Time allocated for rehearsing all sound and technical effects.

(vii) First technical runthrough without costumes or lighting, but *with* sound effects.

(viii) Second technical runthrough with lights and sound, but without costumes or make-up.

(ix) Third technical runthrough, with everything in operation as for the actual performances.

It is a good policy to have two dress rehearsals, one completely private, and one semi-public, perhaps with a specially invited audience.

It is worth stressing that the Director must be fully interested and *appear* to be fully interested in the work of all the various departments working under him. And everyone should feel that he or she is a vital part of the entire enterprise. There cannot be too many conferences or too much comparing of notes. At the end of the production everyone should feel that he has learnt something about *all* the different activities involved.

Also, various people working in the school may well be directly affected by the business of staging the school play even though they do not in any way figure in the artistic or technical preparations for the show and do not necessarily appear on the programme. This will particularly apply to the school caretaker and his various assistants, and to the school cleaning staff. It may well be, for instance, that the scenic designs involve drilling holes in the floor of the stage in order to bolt movable units securely. Since the caretaker is responsible for the maintenance of the school building he should be consulted about this well in advance. Likewise, the mere presentation of the play for evening performances may involve him and others in working overtime. Or the rehearsals may well take up the school hall at the time when the cleaners are supposed to be cleaning it out. In these and any other matters, the people concerned have every right to be consulted *beforehand,* and it is in every one's interests that their sympathy and co-operation should be enlisted right from the start. It is no use proceeding as if nobody in the school existed except those who are dynamically and joyously involved in staging the play.

Drama teachers sometimes have to be informed that caretakers, cleaners and catering staff obey the principles of social psychology just as pupils and teachers do, and they only prove co-operative when they are treated as equal human beings whose views and decisions are of importance to whatever project is in hand.

III Plan into action

The Director: his overall conception of the production

Once the Director has decided on his play or entertainment then he must determine the overall look of his production. If, for instance, he is going to do *The Merchant of Venice* then he may envisage a permanent setting, with no changes being made to the set during the action of the play. So the idea of a composite set will be uppermost in his mind. Generally speaking, the Director will merely be wasting everybody's time if he sets in motion plans for a production before he has thought out this basic conception of what the production is to look like.

If on the other hand the show is a revue or some other kind of extravaganza, then the Director might decide that he wants, for instance, a 'Pop art' setting, with the stage divided into two areas, the proscenium stage and the apron stage, so that he can cut off the main stage at any time simply by closing the main curtains. This enables the Designer to think in terms of scene changes which can take place if needs be outside the view of the audience but while the action of the show continues uninterrupted on the apron.

The Director and Designer: initial conference

The next stage is that the Director will get together with the appointed Designer and present him with his overall conception of the production. Quite probably the Designer will also, by this time, have worked out a basic conception of his own. And perhaps from a fusion of these two basic ideas, the ultimate designs will develop. Certainly, both Director and Designer should be keen to examine and experiment with each other's ideas.

The Designer : getting ideas on to paper

The next stage is for the Designer to start getting his ideas on to paper in the form of sketches and rough ground-plans. From the very beginning the Designer must keep in mind the *exact* limitations of the stage and the auditorium. The Designer may well produce several different basic ideas, all of which should be thought through very carefully and all those should be rejected which simply do not fit sensibly into the limitations of the particular stage. It is remarkable how often designers in the professional theatre as well as in the amateur theatre produce designs which simply cannot be made to work on the particular stage where the production is being mounted. Sometimes the sets are too big even to get on to the stage without actually knocking down one of the four walls of the hall or theatre, or, elaborate revolving sets may be constructed which cannot be revolved without stopping the play for at least fifteen minutes.

After his initial explorings, the Designer may well find that he is left with several ideas, all of which work equally well. So his next task is to go back to the Director and for them both to get down to sorting out which of the ideas should in fact be adopted.

At this stage it is important to note that there is still time for the Director to change his mind, or to find that he needs some extra vital element which he did not at first take into account. Indeed, he may have discovered this as a direct result of his conversations with the Designer.

Although the Designer will not yet have worked out his ideas in detail, he must be clear that they will all work, including not merely the overall idea of the designs but the practical questions involved in that idea. If, for example, he intends to use a flight of steps then he must provide for adequate 'get-off' from the steps. This means that it must be possible for the actors not merely to sweep up the steps but also for them to come down the other side! This may sound absurdly obvious, but it is by no means uncommon for designers to provide magnificent flights of steps which the hero can leap up with superb intention and which leave the hero standing there with nothing better to do than turn round and walk down again. Similarly it is no use having a magnificent pair of double doors if there is no space behind the doors through which actors can make a magnificent entrance.

The Designer : detailed plans

Once the Designer and Director have agreed upon the basic ideas for the sets, the Designer then prepares detailed plans. Working from his rough sketches he now proceeds to draw up a scaled *ground-plan*. This is usually done on a scale of $\frac{1}{2}$ in. to 1 ft. This will show, as viewed from above, not only the shape of the set, but exactly how that set is made up with flats or units of various sizes. Obviously, before this can be done, the Designer must have a ground-plan of the stage itself.

For examples of ground-plans see illustrations 7, and 13 to 19.

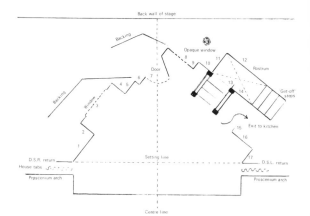

7   *Ground-plan of box-set*

8   *Bird's-eye view of 7, showing returns and backings*

He will next do an *elevation*. This consists of drawings, on the same scale as the ground-plan, of the various flats or units employed in the designs, numbered to correspond with their numbers on the ground-plan. See illustration 9a.

He can also do a 'bird's-eye view' perspective of the designs, based exactly on the ground-plans. This can be very helpful to the Director and to everybody else, for it will show clearly how the set will actually work and how it fits technically into the ground-plan. It is also, for the Designer, a good visual

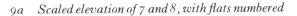

9a   Scaled elevation of 7 and 8, with flats numbered

preliminary to the making of the scale model. See illustrations 8 and 19.

Before making the model there should be a conference for all interested parties, where the designs are explained with the aid of the ground-plans and sketches and where all technical points can be fully thrashed out.

It is from the model, together with the ground-plans and elevations, that the sets will ultimately be made.

The *model* will be on the same scale – $\frac{1}{2}$ in. to 1 ft. This is made from an elevation drawn out on thin show card, as in illustration 9. On the elevation, all the flats are laid out side by side in one long straight line, starting with the downstage right flat, nearest to the proscenium arch, which is numbered One. To each flat is added a flap of extra card to support it when the model is actually 'stood up'. While in this 'elevation' stage, the set is painted in the colours intended for use on the actual stage. Then the designs are cut out and the flaps bent, so that the model can be stood up. It is very useful to have a copy of the ground-plan pinned or glued to a firm base, and to use this as the base on which to place the model, with the ground-plan numbered in the same way as the elevation.

The next step is to make small independent scale models of any additional units, such as pillars, fireplaces, staircases. These are painted and put into position on the model. All backings to doorways or windows, and any 'get-off' steps or rostra must also be incorporated into the model.

Finally, the whole model should be 'fronted' by a simple proscenium arch which is a replica in scale of the proscenium arch opening in the school hall or theatre. This need not be fixed or glued, since it will be necessary to take it away when wishing to study the model in detail.

9b   Elevation of stair unit

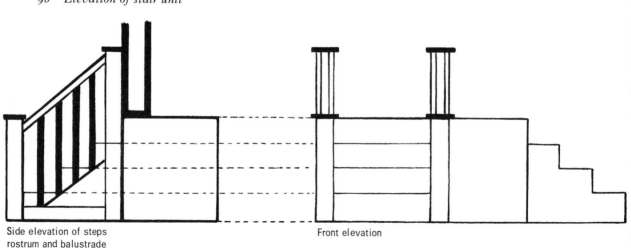

Side elevation of steps
rostrum and balustrade

Front elevation

Sight lines

Before the Designer can finalise his plans, he must consider the question of sight lines. This means that he must work out (a) the maximum area of the stage which any part of the audience will be able to see and (b) the minimum area of the stage which any part of the audience will be able to see.

This will involve (i) masking the sides of the stage with wing flats/curtains so that no part of the audience can see the backstage and similarly masking the area above the stage with borders, and (ii) ensuring that no absolutely vital piece of scenery is invisible to any part of the audience.

As regards (i) the working out of the sight lines is dependent entirely on the arrangement of seating. Generally speaking, the maximum area of the left-hand side of the stage that is visible to the audience is that part of the stage that is visible to a person seated at the end of the front row of the stalls on the right-hand side. And the wing curtains or flats must be so arranged as to obscure completely his line of vision into the backstage. Similarly, the maximum area above the stage that is visible to any part of the audience is that area that is visible to a person seated in the middle of the front row of the stalls, and the borders must be so placed as to ensure that such a person cannot see what the Designer does not want him to see. See illustrations 10 and 11.

As regards (ii) it must be noted that it is not often possible for an entire audience to see *all* of a stage. But it is essential that an entire audience see all major scenic items, and that all the actual acting area of any stage is fully visible.

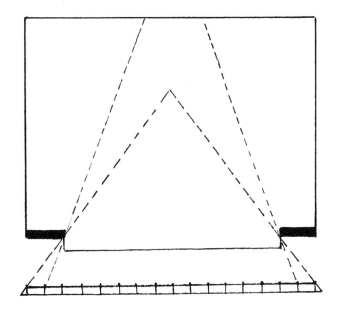

10   *Ground-plan of stage and front row of stalls, showing sight lines in width and showing how the narrowing of rows extends the audience's maximum area of vision*

11   *Sight lines in height*

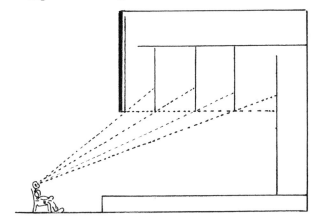

29

Presenting the model

Once the model is completed, a meeting is called for all personnel, and the detailed workings of the sets are explained by the Designer. At this stage, slight adjustments can still be made without having to scrap the entire plan. Hence every department should raise queries affecting their own operations. The Lighting Designer will be able to see for the first time the general task ahead of him. The Stage Manager will be able to note whether there are any complicated scene changes, and how they are to be accomplished. Directors and Designers both have to be told, from time to time, that twenty actors cannot safely be expected to vacate a stage in a 5-second blackout. Nor can a heavy throne be brought on from the wings while actors are trying to get off the stage by the same route. The Stage Manager's job is to see to it that all the scenic and staging ideas that go into the production are genuinely practicable. It is the audience who should be transported to a world of make-believe: those who are creating the make-believe must be solidly matter-of-fact. Entertaining others is a serious business.

Now the work of preparing the actual scenery and staging can commence: everyone should be provided with a copy of the ground-plan, and the model should always be available for reference. Also, the model should be seen by all the actors, so that they have a real visual idea of the settings in which they will perform.

Wardrobe

The Director, Designer and Wardrobe Mistress should meet together to discuss costume requirements in detail. They will have to decide whether costumes are to be hired or made in the school, or whether any costumes are to be provided by the players themselves. Questions of wigs, if any, will have to be discussed. Everything will of course depend on the facilities of the particular school: some schools are equipped with needlework departments which can make superb costumes specially for the drama production, and where the whole business of choosing colours, materials and styles can be thrashed out and incorporated into the initial conception of the production. Other schools consider themselves lucky if they are able to spend £10 on the hire of costumes. Obviously this whole question will dictate to a considerable extent the actual choice of show.

A few general comments may be made here about costumes:

(i) *The actor and the costume.* Costume Designers and Directors often have brilliant ideas for costumes which are quite unrelated to the specific actors who are going to have to wear them. No actor should ever wear any costume in which he in any way feels or looks uncomfortable. The one exception to this, is in the case of costumes provided for characters who are specifically meant, by the dramatist, to wear costumes which make them look in some way absurd. But even this will not necessarily mean wearing a costume which highlights the actor's physical shortcomings. If the audience titter when an actor walks on stage in his costume, this is not because the audience is 'uneducated' or 'ill-mannered': it is because the Director and the Costume Designer, together or separately, have lacked the basic good sense to work out in advance what type of clothing particular players can happily wear. There are no absolute rules: some young men both look and feel splendid if dressed in tights; others feel awkward and gauche and look as uncomfortable as they feel. Some young ladies, asked to dress as Elizabethan males for a girls' school production of, say, *The Taming of the Shrew,* are able to carry off their roles with tremendous verve and conviction. Others simply cannot do it. This is something that the Director must be able to anticipate. He must guarantee that none of his players will ever be made ridiculous by appearing in his production.

The Director and the Costume Designer should be willing to make discreet departures from historical accuracy if in so doing, they make the actor feel at home with his costume. If an actor has thinnish legs, for instance, and he has to wear tights, do not also ask him to wear ballet-type slippers. Give him a solid-looking pair of boots and a good cloak – these will help his movement and his general appearance.

(ii) *Line and shape of costumes.* A good costume hangs well. It looks comfortable. It has what we call good 'line'. And its shape is right for that particular character, whether she be Audrey in *As You Like It,* or Rosalind.

(iii) *Material.* Of all materials wool jersey and velveteen are probably the best, though they are fairly expensive. Cheap satin can also be useful, especially in large quantities, as in a flowering skirt, where it will look very effective. All these materials light well, as does shot silk.

Fine hessian is useful for costumes which have to be painted, say with some heraldic design. Nylon can be especially useful as it is easily washable, and does not have to be ironed, but be careful of the period of costume for which any material, and especially nylon, is being used: nylon, for instance, is easily recognisable on a stage and hence might be wrong in, say, an eighteenth-century play where you are striving for a realistic effect.

Cheap cotton can be used provided it is possible to iron all costumes between one performance and the next.

Avoid using shiny-surfaced materials, and avoid all *very* expensive materials – not only because of the expense, but also because the 'richness' will not usually notice on the stage.

Programmes, handbills, tickets, publicity

The design of these items can be handled by the Designer's assistants, working in consultation with the Designer and the Director. It may be a good idea to have a single motif running through all publicity, including the tickets and the programmes. All these items must strike the right note, summing up and evoking the atmosphere and spirit of the production.

Handbills are an excellent way of spreading information about the show – but they should try to say too little rather than too much. If produced within the school they can be virtually costless. Professional printers charge about £10 per thousand for a simple, two-sided, one-colour handbill, and anything from £25 upwards for a more ambitious project. But if your budget permits you to experiment in this field, or if your school facilities allow it to be done inside the school, then the results can be very impressive, and the drawing-power of a good handbill can be quite considerable. They have to be available in large quantities, in order that they can be sent off to possibly interested parties – including schools, clubs and organisations, as well as individuals, and in order that they can be spread around and handed about as needs be.

In the designing of programmes and the layout of the contents, careful attention should be given to the question of who is to be mentioned. Quite often programme designers settle for some statement such as:

'We should like to thank all parents and staff who have assisted in this production' – which is of no interest to the reader, says nothing whatsoever about the production and is an extremely ungenerous way of giving thanks to the anonymous ladies and gentlemen referred to. Even worse is that awful old adage:

'We should like to thank all those people, too numerous to mention. . . .' – which always implies that there have been vast regiments of helpers, many of whom could happily have been dispensed with.

The best policy is not to 'thank' people, but to state simply the particular job they have done. If Mrs X has been a useful member of the wardrobe crew, then she should be included in the list of wardrobe assistants. In this way the audience sees something of the dimensions of the project, and this of itself is interesting.

The programme should also include some form of introduction to the play, written by the Production Manager or member of the cast, and aimed at putting the audience in the right mood before the play begins. Also, if there are any forthcoming productions in other schools in the area, give them some form of free advertisement in your programme. This is excellent for public relations and in the long run, when the habit spreads, it provides free publicity for everyone.

IV A basic approach to stage design

Basic types of design

We may divide the different kinds of stage design into the following, starting with the simplest:

(i) *The bare stage*. An effective setting, in fact, and one which concentrates all attention upon the actors, the lighting and the costumes.

(ii) *Independent stages* made up of steps, rostra and ramps.

(iii) *Curtain sets,* i.e. a bare stage dressed with curtains suspended in the wings and across the back of the stage. See illustration 12a. The curtains should be black, dark blue or grey, but never oatmeal or pink, as these tend to make the actors' faces merge into the background.

A minor variation on the same idea is to use flats instead of curtains.

(iv) *Painted backcloth and cut-out wings* – this is the same as the previous design, except that there is a painted backcloth at the back of the stage instead of a plain curtain, and instead of the plain flats or curtains hanging in the wings, simple cut-out flats are used to represent some kind of actual scenery. See illustration 12b. This kind of design is nowadays most closely associated with pantomime and operetta.

12a *Curtain set*

12b *Painted backcloth and cut-out wings*

34

(v) *Simple designs with flats*—illustrations 13a, b, c and d, show simple variations on a set made up with flats, and illustration 13e shows the ground-plan for all four.

13a

13a–d   Variations of simple flat sets

13b   With painted backing

13c

13d

13e Ground-plan for 13a–d

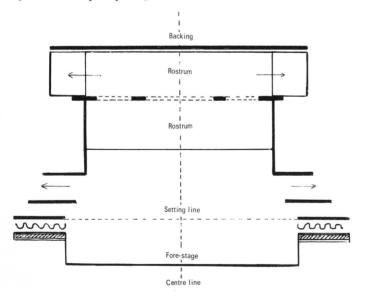

Backing

Rostrum

Rostrum

Setting line

Fore-stage

Centre line

(vi) *Simple box-set.* Illustration 14 shows the ground-plan for a simple box-set. The walls are slightly perspected to give an illusion of greater depth. One should avoid straight walls on a stage, and hence the walls in this illustration are broken up by the door, window and fireplace. But where space permits, the best way to break up long straight walls is by angling and recessing, as the next illustrations show. The set in this illustration is of course ideal for a small stage.

One basic idea for a box-set can easily be adapted to different stages: illustration 15 shows the ground-plan for a simple box-set depicting the interior of a cottage, designed for a stage which has plenty of width but very little depth.

Illustration 16 shows the same set adapted to a stage of equal width but of greater depth. This allows the set to be expanded and to become much more interesting. The whole additional upstage area is mounted on a platform, say 1 ft high, to create a more varied effect, and this is shown on the ground-plan by a dotted line.

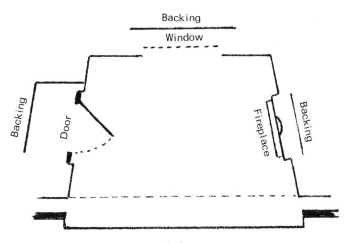

14   *Ground-plan for a simple box-set*

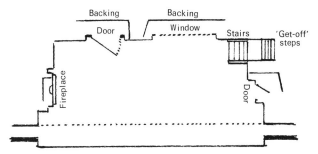

15   *Adaptation of 14 to a shallow but wide stage*

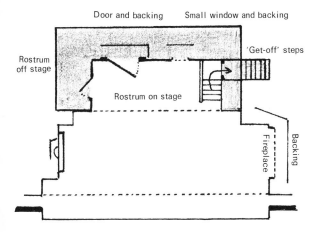

16   *Adaptation of 14 to a wide and deep stage*

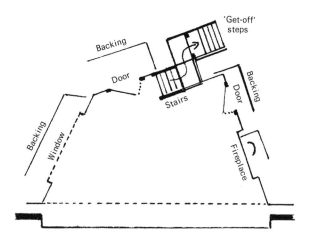

17 *Adaptation of 14 into a more novel shape*

Illustration 17 shows the same set angled in a more novel fashion, and in such a way as to ensure that all the audience see all its details.

Illustration 18 shows the same set adapted to a narrower stage. Angling the walls in this way not only makes the set more interesting to look at, but also allows much more wing space.

Illustration 19 is a simple sketch of the ground-plan in illustration 15, of which the other ground-plans are variations. Illustration 20 shows an additional way of breaking up a box-set so as to avoid the monotony of long straight lines of adjacent flats.

18 *Adaptation of 14 to a narrow stage*

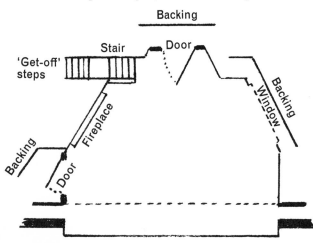

19   *Rough sketch, showing bird's-eye view elevation of 15*

20   *Additional way of breaking up a box-set*

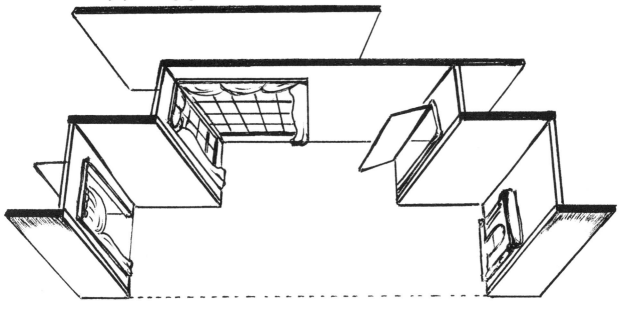

(vii) *Cyclorama*. This can be used most effectively in combination with a simple stylised setting, as in illustration 21. It can also be used in combination with various pieces of cut-out flats, as in illustration 22, or in combination with draped curtains, as in illustration 23.

Illustration 24 shows the use of black curtains in place of the cyclorama.

21   Cyclorama with simple stylised setting

23   Cyclorama with draped curtains

22   Cyclorama with cut-out flats

24   Black curtains used instead of cyclorama

(viii) *Three-dimensional units built on trucks* – these are highly adaptable and useful forms of scenery. It is possible to conceive an entire design in terms of one revolving unit which as it revolves reveals, say, three completely different settings. Or interesting effects can be achieved with a pair of revolves, which can be manipulated separately and together. Note that these units have to be bolted to the floor if they are to be stable, and that they have to be bolted in two different places – so that one bolt can be undone to swing the revolve round to a new position, while the revolve is pivoted by the other bolt.

The effect of even the simplest revolving three-dimensional unit can be quite spectacular, especially if it is moved in full view of the audience: the one side of the unit may, for instance, represent the interior of a house and the opposite the exterior, while a second unit may join up with it to form part of the interior, and it is then separated from the first unit when they are both revolved, the second one then becoming, for instance, the shop on the other side of the road.

Alternatively double-sided cut-out flats can be built on trucks, and moved around the stage in the same way.

Usually the ideal background for your truck units is the cyclorama.

V Stage lighting

General principles

1 Remember that your prime function is to light the actors, not to light the scenery or the stage.

2 Time must be allowed for re-thinking. No matter how well you work out your lighting in advance, you will probably find there has to be quite an amount of readjustment when the scenery and the lights have actually been set up.

3 Lighting is affected by the colour of your set. If the overall colour is a pale one, then this will create the effect, when a lot of lights are on it, of a very hot stage, and the glare can sometimes bounce back on the audience. This in turn will make the actors' faces appear to be poorly defined and to merge into the background.

4 On the other hand a dark set will never look brilliant no matter how much light you concentrate upon it. But the actors will look very vivid indeed, because they will be so sharply defined by the dark background. In fact, on a dark set you can obtain splendid effects with just a couple of spots.

5 Your stage floor-covering must never be at all shiny.

6 In lighting an open stage you will have to rely on front-of-house lights exclusively, and the difficulty may well be where to hang or stand them. Generally it is no use simply to place them on their stands on the floor, because even if you extend the stands to their maximum height, they may still not be high enough. If actors are playing on a raised platform of say, 2 feet in height, then your lowest standing spot should ideally be 14 feet

from the ground, though you may be able to get away with 12 feet for some, though not for all of the spots. For reasons such as this, it is essential that the Lighting Designer is brought into the conferences at the earliest stages of planning.

7 Remember that any scenery painted dead white, and lit without colour filters, will automatically be the brightest thing on the stage. This may well be exactly what you want, but be very careful. Be especially careful of creating completely white sets.

8 The ideal colour for stage drapes/curtains is black, dark blue or grey.

9 The most satisfactory way to light actors is by *directional lighting*. This involves the use chiefly of spotlights, but in combination with a very judicious and sparing use of floodlights. To light well a moderately sized stage it is not essential to have a large number of lights to work with. A good lighting plan can be devised with ten spots and a couple of floods.

10 In general, the centre and upstage areas of the stage are illuminated by lights hanging above, or standing on, the stage. The downstage and forestage are illuminated by lights suspended from the front-of-house.

11 Lights can either be suspended from bars or wall-brackets, or supported on stands. Occasionally it is useful to put the stands on boxes in order to achieve added height for the source of light.

25   *The acting areas of the stage*

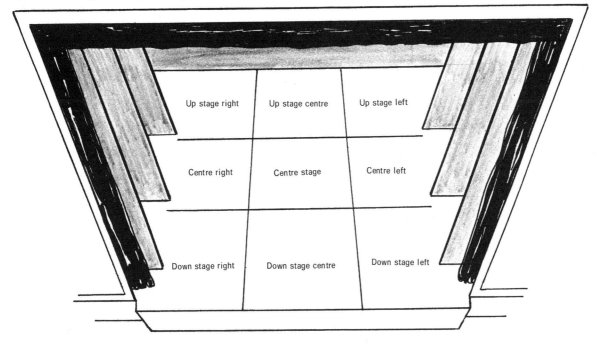

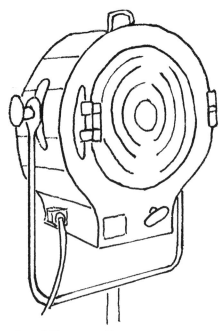

26a   *Mirror-profile spot*

The different kinds of stage lighting

There are two kinds:
Spotlights. These illuminate a well-defined area. There are three kinds of spotlight:
(i) Mirror-profile spot. See illustration 26a. This has a hard-edged beam. Different shapes can be placed in the gate between the reflector and the lens, and by this means any shape of spot can be produced, such as circular, semicircular or oblong.
(ii) Focus lantern. See illustration 26b. This does not give a small clear-cut spot, but lights a more general area. It is in fact half-way between a spot and a flood.
(iii) Fresnal spot. See illustration 26c. This produces an adjustable semicircular spot and it can therefore be used to illuminate a small or large area. The light is most intense at the centre of its beam, and it is soft-edged. Of the three kinds of spotlight it is the most subtle in its effect, and the most useful.
Small spotlights are known as 'baby' spots.

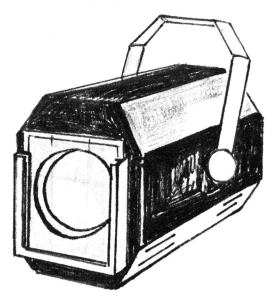

26b   *Focus lantern*

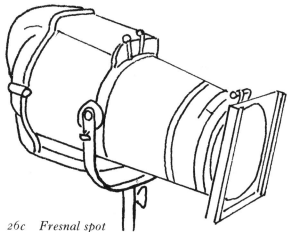

26c   *Fresnal spot*

Floodlights. These illuminate large areas, but they do not have a directional beam and they therefore give diffuse rather than specific lighting. Consequently one uses spotlights to light the actors, and floodlights are used either to light the backcloth or cyclorama, or to give an added lift to a scene where bright illumination is called for.

Floodlights may either be single floods – see illustration 27a – or groups of floods encased in long rectangular boxes and called battens – see illustration 27b.

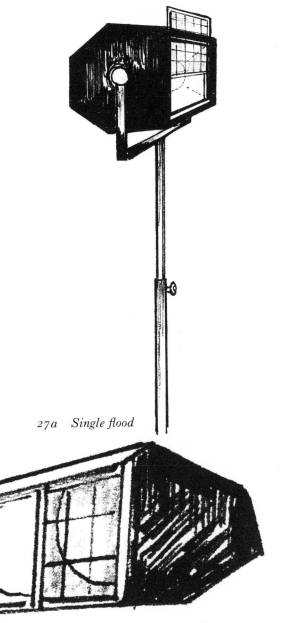

27a   Single flood

27b   Batten

An approach to stage lighting

Stage lighting can be approached in this simple progression:

(i) *Illuminating the actors with a single spotlight directed at the centre stage*

Illustration 28a shows two actors illuminated in a single spot. This allows them to be seen but gives them little freedom of movement. The light is hung from the Number One Spot Bar. This is the bar which hangs immediately behind the proscenium arch. Lights hung from this bar can only illuminate actors when they are centre stage or upstage. If lights hung from this bar are aimed downstage then they merely light up the tops of the actors' heads.

28a   Single spot directed at centre stage

(ii) *Illuminating the actors with a small group of spotlights directed at the centre stage*

Illustration 28b shows the addition of two spots, hanging stage left and stage right respectively on the Number One Spot Bar. Notice that the spots are so directed that their light overlaps. This has to be experimented with until an even spread of light is obtained.

Illustrations 31 and 32 suggest a fuller version of the same basic idea: they show a ground-plan and elevation of centre and upstage lighting using five spots hanging from the Number One Spot Bar.

(iii) *Illuminating the actors in the downstage area with spots hanging from the front-of-house*

Illustration 28c shows the illumination of the downstage area by the use of two pairs of spots suspended from either side of the front-of-house. If you add to this the lights suspended from the Number One Spot Bar in the previous illustrations you will have the principal acting areas fairly well covered. If you have in reserve a couple of spots to give extra lift when needed, then you are quite well provided for. Obviously the wider and deeper the stage, the more light will be needed to cover it.

(iv) *Lighting the actors on the apron*

Much the same principle applies as with lighting the downstage area. Use a couple of spots at each side of the front-of-house and a large spot from the centre of the hall, hanging from a bar or balcony. If you have neither bar nor balcony you can still cover the apron quite adequately from the sides. Illustration 29 shows a ground-plan for lighting the apron.

Illustration 30 shows an elevation of the ground-plan in illustration 29.

28b   *Group of spots directed at centre stage*

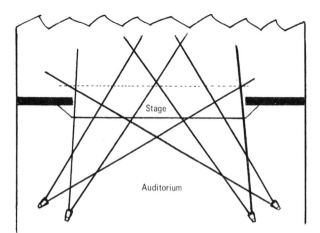

28c   Lighting the downstage

28d   Elevation of 28c

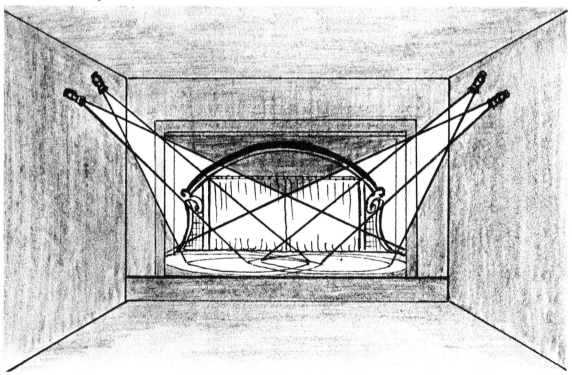

48

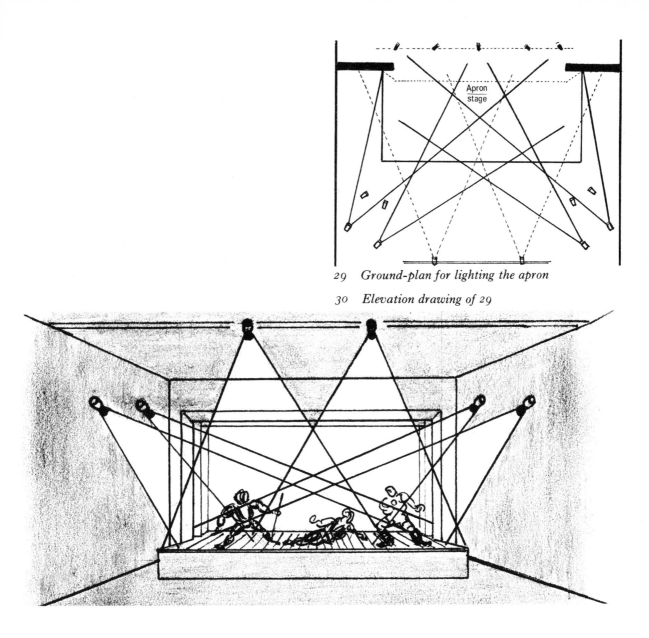

29 *Ground-plan for lighting the apron*

30 *Elevation drawing of 29*

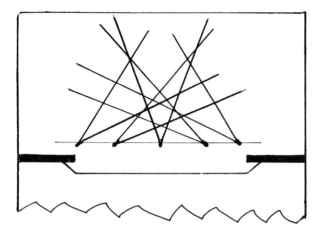

31, 32 *Extended or more sophisticated versions of 28a and 28b*

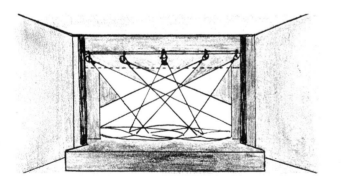

(v) *Lighting the actors in the upstage area*
If you use the upstage area for acting purposes then you will probably need some additional lighting. This can be achieved simply by adding two spots to the Number One Spot Bar, hanging respectively one-third and two-thirds of the way across, and with their beams crossing and aimed at the upstage area. On a larger stage you would use the Number Two Spot Bar, i.e. the bar hanging farther upstage and towards the centre stage.

(vi) *Lighting the cyclorama*
If you are using the cyclorama to create an illusion of sky then the best way to do this is by hanging a set of batten lighting from the top of the stage at least 3 feet from the cyclorama, using two or three lengths of 6 feet each, and placing the same amount along the floor in front of the cyclorama and at the same distance. If the stage is quite a small one then you can create the same effect with a couple of individual floods. If your stage is equipped with floodlights then this is a better use for them than it is to leave them in front of the main curtains, for you will be able to light your actors quite effectively with spots and without using the floodlights at all.

When you use battens for lighting the cyclorama you should use wide-angled reflectors in each compartment. If your battens are so circuited that three or four different colours can be used separately, then use one circuit of open white, one circuit of steel and one circuit of deep blue, and mix them until you get the colour you want.

(vii) *Lighting the backings*
Many stage sets have backings. These are views seen through, say, windows or doors. They can consist of a painted backcloth, or a painted flat, or a portion of the cyclorama.

These have to be lit quite independently of the rest of the stage. Floodlighting is usually the simplest answer, using either single floods or battens.

(viii) *Use of colour filters*

Stage lighting is aided by the use of different colour filters, in the form of gelatine or plastic sheets, which can be fitted in front of spots or floods. These have standard names and numbers. There are about sixty different colours, but the most useful are

Number 3	Straw
Number 17	Steel blue
Number 18	Light blue
Number 50	Pale yellow
Number 52	Pale gold
Number 53	Pale salmon
Number 54	Pale rose
Frost filter	

In using colour filters, note:

The deeper the colour the less light you get. Open white is the maximum brightness possible.

Frost filters are a boon where the edges of the spot's focus are too hard. The frost filter helps to soften them. If you do not wish to lose the power of the light, then a hole can be cut into the centre of the gelatine.

The frost filter can be used in combination with any other filters. The frost filter itself is of course neutral, like frosted glass.

A mixing of 50, 52, 53 and 54 will usually give the right kind of balance to the acting area – i.e. using 50 in say one pair of spots, 52 in another.

As a rule, keep off the deep or the hot colours such as purple, orange or red. Use 17 – steel blue – for hard brightness or moonlight.

If you want the real colour of costumes to be brought out, only use the palest colour filters, otherwise the colours on stage will disappear into an overall muddiness.

Working out the stage lighting

Designing the lighting for a show is usually done quite early in the stages of production. Obviously, if you are lighting a straightforward comedy in which all the action takes place in the drawing-room in the daytime, then you will need very cheerful lighting throughout, though you may need to have a couple of spots in reserve if, say, you are doing a play which in the last act switches to a sunlit garden.

When you come to plays where the location and moods vary then of course much more experiment is possible. Remember that in lighting, as in anything else on stage, contrast is the key word. Vary your lighting at every plausible opportunity. Do *not* start the play with all the lights you have, unless this is essential. Vary also the areas which you illuminate. It can be most effective, for instance, to depict the approach of night by slowly fading the lights on the upstage and centre areas until only the apron or downstage areas are left illuminated. This is more effective than simply dimming everything.

Also, remember that you can contrast different intensities of light, as well as contrasting total blackout and light.

If you are lighting a revue or music hall, then you may find it very useful to have one spot which is manually directed in the course of the show to follow specific performers.

Here again, you should vary your lighting from one number to the next.

Once the lighting plot has been provisionally agreed on, the Lighting Designer prepares ground-plans of the lighting so that the Director can see precisely those areas which are illuminated. See illustrations 28c, 29 and 31.

33a   Showing in profile the need for lights to over-lap in order to obtain an even spread of light

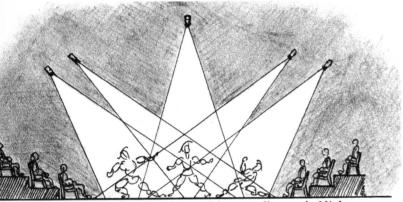

33b   Showing need for overall spread of light on an arena stage while being careful not to light the audience

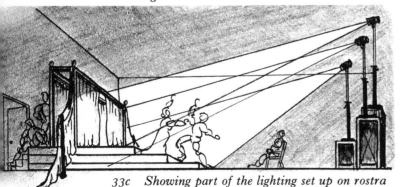

33c   Showing part of the lighting set up on rostra

33d   Showing the atmospheric effectiveness of a single spot

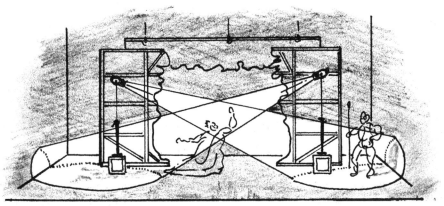

33e   Cross-lighting from wings

33f   Atmospheric effectiveness of two spots

Setting up the lights

Each spot and each flood has to be set separately. The Lighting Director will need at least three assistants. The first assistant positions the light, the second assistant sits at the switchboard, and the third assistant moves across the stage in the various areas of light so that the Lighting Director can see whether the lights are in the right position and at the right angle. The third assistant should be as tall as the tallest member of the acting company.

Colour filters are placed inside each light as soon as it is satisfactorily positioned. Usually the first lights to be set are those on the Number One Spot Bar, followed by those on the Number Two Spot Bar. Then the front-of-house lights are fixed. Lights on the cyclorama and lights on backings are left until last. Each light is positioned individually, first against a background of complete darkness, and then in conjunction with the other lights. The process is normally a lengthy one and you need to do quite a lot of rearranging before the lights can be permanently fixed.

Operating the lights

This can be done in two ways:
(i) The Lighting Director sits out front, at the back of the hall, where he has his own control box from which he controls all the lights. In this case he simply gives all necessary instructions directly to his assistants. Alternatively, where the lighting controls are backstage, the Designer may still have a box from which he watches the action of the play and from which he is connected by intercom with his backstage staff.

(ii) All the lighting equipment is backstage and so are the Lighting Director and his assistants. It is worth adding that this is not as good a system as (i), especially where the lighting plot is quite complicated.

Usually the Lighting Director gives his assistants the cues for the changes of lighting in two stages. All the lighting cues are numbered so that the assistants operating the lights simply follow the list of numbers with the details of the operations to be performed at each lighting cue. First he gives the cue 'Get ready for Number 8' a minute or so before the Number 8 lighting cue is actually imminent, and then he gives the cue 'Go Number 8' at the appropriate moment.

Lighting the sections of the acting area

The elementary approach to stage lighting suggested earlier in this chapter looked at the problems in terms of lighting first the centre stage, then the downstage, then the apron and then the upstage. This is of course a simplification, especially where large stages are concerned where there will be a wider acting area than can be split up into the conventional divisions of upstage, centre stage and downstage. But the same basic principle will still apply: think of your entire acting area in terms of sections and then proceed to light each section, using as a general guide the policy of employing two spots to light each section with each spot aimed from a more or less opposite direction and thus creating a degree of overspill.

Front-of-house lights

The problem with the front-of-house lights (spots or floods) if there is no permanent fixture provided, is where to put them. There is also the problem of being able to place them high enough. If it is possible to fix a grid or bracket either to the side walls or to some other convenient structure, then the lights can be hung from this. A balcony going round the hall can be useful for this purpose, and even if it is not possible to fix brackets to the balcony, at least the lights can be put on stands on the balcony.

It may well be, in the end, that all the f.o.h. lights have to be on stands, and that the problem then is to get adequate height while at the same time ensuring that the stands cannot in any way be moved by the audience. Stout tables can be useful for this purpose, as also can rostra. It is worth noting that although the problem can be a difficult one, touring companies who go round visiting schools and halls have to cope with it all the time. But it is essential that, if any light has to be left within reach of the audience, someone stout and reliable is left in charge of it.

It is important to note that where a light is hung from the *centre* of the hall/theatre, then lack of height is more damaging than in the case of light coming from the sides.

Finally, it is worth repeating the basic principle we referred to at the beginning of this chapter: when you light an area of the stage you are lighting *the actor* in that area and NOT the floor of the stage. Therefore the centre of the beam of light will NOT hit the floor of the illuminated area: it will be directed at the head and shoulders of the actors standing or sitting there.

VI Building

Flats

Most scenery, however complex the setting may appear, will in fact be made up of small units. The most commonly used of these small units are flats – a neat and lightweight theatrical construction made from wood and canvas. The wood is usually 3 in. wide and 1 in. thick. It is cut to the required lengths and the pieces are then assembled to make a frame on which to stretch, nail and glue the canvas.

The frame of a flat essentially consists of:

Two vertical lengths of wood known as the stiles;

Two horizontal lengths of wood known as the rails;

A central cross-piece or rail;

A piece angled at 45 degrees across one of the corners in order to keep the true shape of the flat.

See illustration 34a.

Obviously, the bigger the flat, the more cross rails and stiles will be needed for strengthening.

Joints. Several different joints can be used. The most useful and most used one is the *mortice and tenon joint,* with the mortice in the rail and the tenon in the stile. See illustration 34b. This enables the weight of the stile to sit on the shoulder of the rail. The base of the flat then has only one surface, that of the underside of the rail in contact with the floor. This is important, for the correct way to move a flat is to slide it along the floor. You do not lift it bodily.

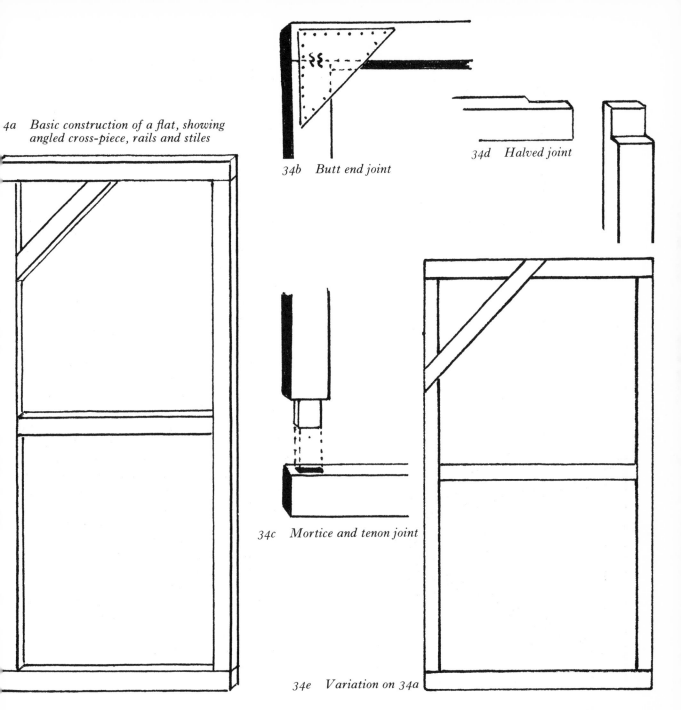

4a   *Basic construction of a flat, showing angled cross-piece, rails and stiles*

34b   *Butt end joint*

34d   *Halved joint*

34c   *Mortice and tenon joint*

34e   *Variation on 34a*

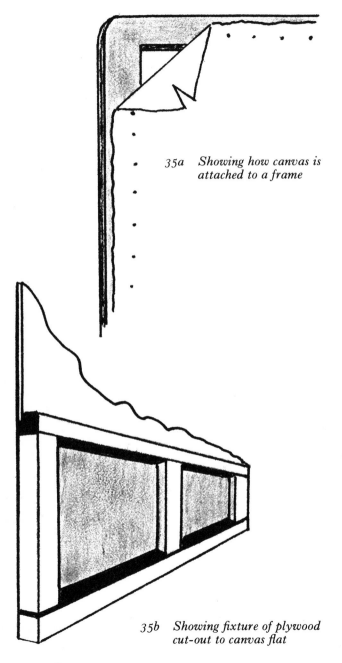

35a *Showing how canvas is attached to a frame*

35b *Showing fixture of plywood cut-out to canvas flat*

The central rail also should be a mortice and tenon joint.

In general the mortice and tenon joint should be used wherever the flat is quite a large one. With smaller units then a simpler joint such as the *butt end* joint (see illustration 34c) or the *halved joint* (see illustration 34d) can be used.

The whole frame is then *glued and screwed*. Use hot glue, of course, and remember to see that as the glue is brushed on, it starts to foam. You are then sure that it will stick. Then set in the screws at each corner – at least three screws in each corner. The glue will take at least 24 hours to set.

The canvas is usually sold in bales, 36 in. or 72 in. wide. After cutting to the required length, tack down the canvas on one of the shorter sides of the flat. The canvas does not overlap but meets the outer edge of the wooden stile or rail, and the tacks are set on the inner edge. The loose bit of canvas all round the outer edge is lifted for the glue to be applied.

The tacking process is repeated on the other three inner edges of the flat and you must be sure to stretch the canvas as tightly as possible. When all edges have been tacked the glue is applied to the wood and the canvas is securely smoothed down over the glued wood. Be sure to eliminate any rucks or creases. A rag dipped in hot water and then squeezed out, can be used for this purpose.

In each of the four corners of the canvas make a small triangular cut about $1\frac{1}{2}$ in. long and 1 in. wide, using a razor or sharp knife. See illustration 35a which shows how canvas is attached to a frame, and illustration 35b which shows the fixture of a plywood cut-out to the canvas flat. The small triangular cut helps the corners to lie easily.

The flat should now be really taut, and ready for the prime coat of size and whitening.

Window, fireplace and door flats are constructed in exactly the same way, except that with a door flat the rail at the base, across the opening, is cut short, and an iron sill is fixed. This applies also to french windows and arches.

A door flat is a flat constructed with an opening into which the door is fitted. There are two kinds of door-fitting techniques:

(a) To hinge a door, whether a wooden one, or one made of wood and canvas, into the aperture of the flat.

(b) To make a completely independent door unit consisting of a wooden door frame with a wooden door hinged to it. The entire unit is slotted into the waiting aperture of the door flat and to the flat by a hinged flap brace.

The second is the more favoured technique because it is three dimensional.

See illustrations 36–8.

Book flats. If a large expanse of wall is required, say more than 6 feet, then the best way to achieve this is to hinge two flats together to form a book flat. The hinges are placed on the canvased sides of the two flats and the join and hinges are covered by a strip of canvas glued down the whole length of the fold (or join) of the two flats.

They are then ready for painting.

This technique is also useful where a large opening or arch is required, the centre point of the arch being the joining of the two frames. Alternatively, it is possible to construct a large opening in three sections: two upright plain flats are attached or hinged on to either side of an arch cross-piece, a smaller flat – perhaps a piece 8 ft by 1½ ft. This method, or any variation of it, is useful for constructing

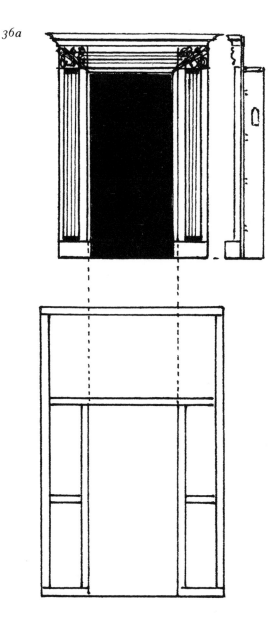

36a

36a, b, c *Showing door flat, window flat and fireplace flat, together with the appropriate units which slot into them*

59

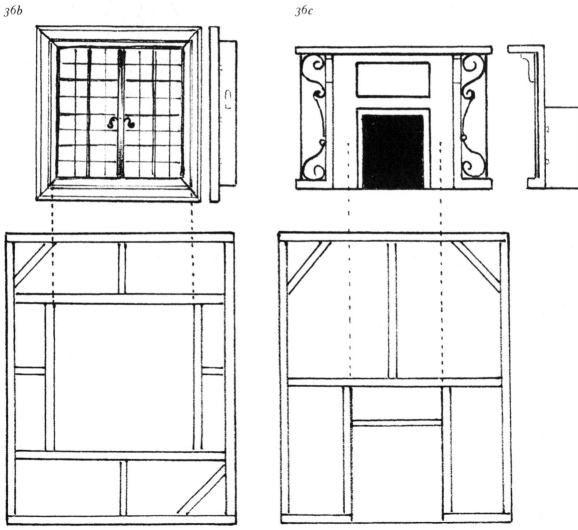

a small false proscenium. See illustration 44a.

It is worth noting that if the structure has to be fairly large and if it proves to be rather top-heavy, then it is advisable to have it secured with ropes or nylon wire hanging from suitable anchorage above. This will take some of the strain, and together with the necessary bracing at stage floor level, will make for greater firmness.

The different forms of *bracing* are shown in illustrations 39a to f.

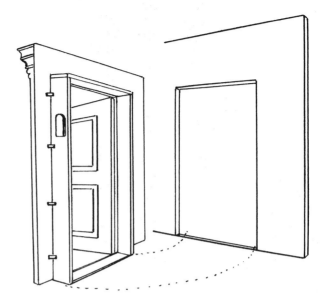

37 *Shows more detailed door unit which slots into door flat*

38 *Shows how flats interlock to avoid light coming through from backstage*

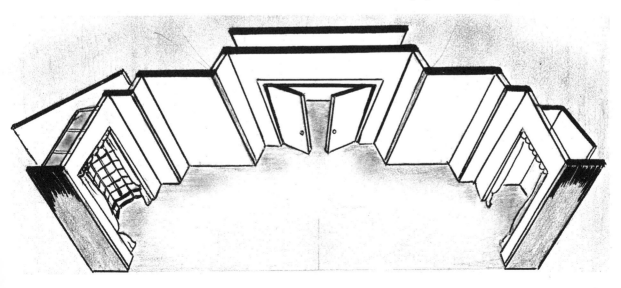

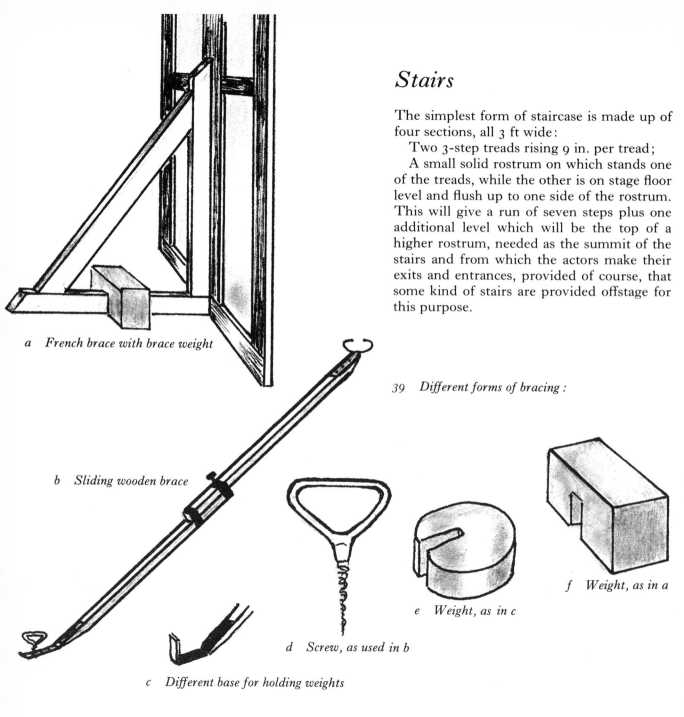

Stairs

The simplest form of staircase is made up of four sections, all 3 ft wide:

Two 3-step treads rising 9 in. per tread;

A small solid rostrum on which stands one of the treads, while the other is on stage floor level and flush up to one side of the rostrum. This will give a run of seven steps plus one additional level which will be the top of a higher rostrum, needed as the summit of the stairs and from which the actors make their exits and entrances, provided of course, that some kind of stairs are provided offstage for this purpose.

a   French brace with brace weight

39   *Different forms of bracing :*

b   Sliding wooden brace

d   Screw, as used in b

e   Weight, as in c

f   Weight, as in a

c   Different base for holding weights

If a really splendid staircase is required, it may be easier and better to have the whole staircase made in one piece, on the same principle as the real-life article, rather than to work at building up several units. In the case of a banister, whether simple or complex, it will in most cases be more straightforward if it is created independently of the staircase itself, and is then pin-hinged to the stairs or affixed more firmly by screws or nails.

But it is always advisable to think first in terms of small units because over a period of time they are more useful. If, for instance, you build up a flight of stairs from separate units, then these three separate units may be of use the following year in the next production, but in a quite different way. Whereas with a major construction it may be difficult if not impossible to use it again, even presuming you are able to store it.

Rostra

Rostra are fascinating units. In their assorted variety they can be pressed into service in many different ways – as steps or balconies or staircases, for instance, or as abstract shapes and different levels which create the mood and atmosphere of a production. The school drama society may be fortunate enough to have a good collection of rostra already in its possession, and sufficient to build up an improvised stage or a complete apron stage or upper stage. The most useful sizes of rostra are 6 ft × 3 ft × 2 ft/1½ ft. With only four of these a small stage of 12 ft × 6 ft can be created, and with an additional pair, a practical inner/upper stage can be created for the production of say, a Restoration Comedy, along the lines discussed in Chapter VIII.

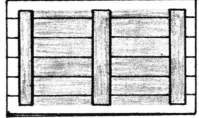

40   *Rostra : two kinds of collapsible rostra*

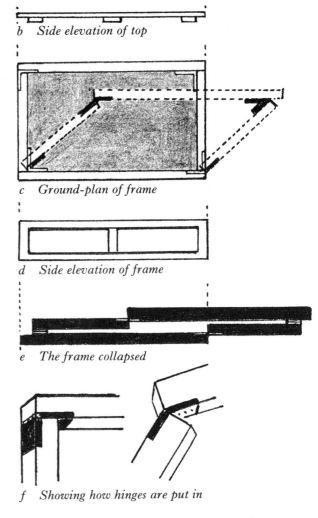

a   Underside of independent rostrum top

b   Side elevation of top

c   Ground-plan of frame

d   Side elevation of frame

e   The frame collapsed

f   Showing how hinges are put in

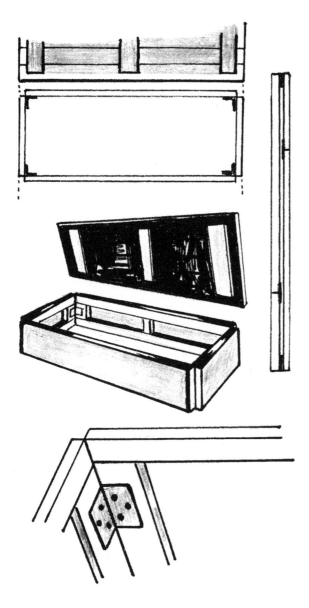

If the rostra are made within the school, then the sides of the rostra can be frames covered in 3-ply. The top can be made of planking 1 ft × 6 ft or $\frac{3}{4}$ in 5-ply board covering the entire area. The larger the surface area the more support will be needed, with some support at roughly $2\frac{1}{2}$ ft intervals.

Collapsible rostra are very useful, especially for transportation or where storage space is at a minimum. The frame is held together by hinges, and the top secures the shape.

See illustrations 40a to g.

All rostra and steps should first be covered with felt, over which canvas is stretched and nailed down and painted with a mixture of scene paint and size. If this is not done they will reverberate as the actors move across them. The size is important because it helps to stop the scene paint from rubbing off or flaking. Sometimes emulsion paint is used. The felt and canvas carpeting also gives the actor a feeling of safety and he therefore does not have to worry about the possibility of slipping.

With the collapsible rostra the canvasing either extends to the ends of the top surface or it is bound round the edge and affixed by tacking to the underside.

With fixed shape rostra, either just the top is canvased, and the sides are left in their 3-ply state, or the canvas is stretched right over the sides and glued down to the bottom edge of the rostrum. Great care will have to be taken with the consequent overlap of canvas at the corners, either by judicious cutting of the material or by neat tucking.

g   *Another kind of collapsible rostrum with different hinging*

Trucks

Trucks are usually constructed on low movable rostra mounted on castors. The castors are hidden by the surrounding lip or sides of the rostrum.

The most practical kind of castor is the swivel castor, which allows the unit to move in any direction. Use silent castors – i.e. rubber-tyred ones, even though they are more expensive. A truck which is, say, 6 feet in length should have six castors: a pair at each end and a pair in the middle.

Fixed-direction castors are useful where a unit is moved in front of the audience.

The sides of trucks must not touch the stage. Their whole purpose is to move across the stage without having to be lifted. If the sides are, say, $\frac{1}{2}$ in. above the floor, then the resulting gap will hardly be noticeable from the front-of-house.

Profile scenery

This is scenery to which an extra piece is attached in the shape of some kind of cut-out.

Illustration 41a shows an upstanding flat with a profile edge.

Illustration 41b shows a long run of scenery, known as a ground-row, with a cut-out edge.

41 *Profile scenery*

a *Standing independently, with french brace*

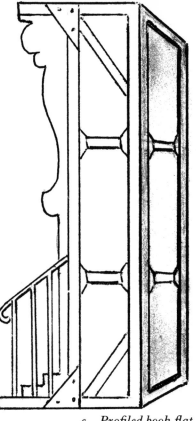

Illustration 41c shows a profiled book flat.

On the edge of the flat which requires to have the profiled plywood attached, a $\frac{1}{2}$-in. groove is cut on the side where the flat is to be canvased, the depth of the groove being the thickness of the 3-ply cut-out piece. This is glued and tacked firmly into the flat. Then, if the flat is newly constructed, canvas can be stretched, glued and tacked in one piece over both the plywood profile and the frame to which it is attached. Then it is ready for priming. If it is an older flat that is already canvased and the profile piece is attached, then a strip of canvas is glued over the join.

Independent profile pieces can be made completely of plywood, or the main construction can be a wood and canvas frame to the edges of which is attached the profiled shape. The same method of grooving and attachment is employed as described above.

c Profiled book flat

b Profiled ground row

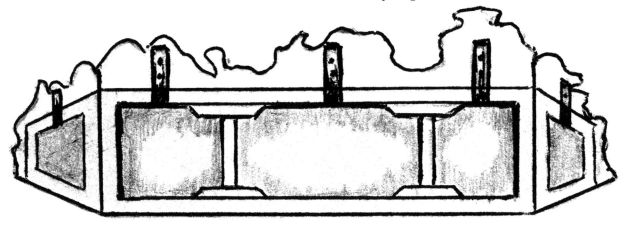

VII Painting

Basic points

There must be good co-operation between the Director, the Scenic Designer and the Lighting Designer.

(i) *Colour filters*. Where colour filters are being used it is a good idea to make up odd pieces of canvas painted with the same colours as are to be used on the sets, and then to throw light on to the pieces of canvas while experimenting with various colour filters. In this way you can see how the colour of the sets is going to be affected by the particular filters which you eventually decide to use.

(ii) *Experiment*. It is important to experiment with all the various paints or mixtures of paints before actually applying them to the scenery. Try the paints first on some canvas samples. This is necessary because scene paint creates a lighter colour when it has dried than it does in liquid form in the bucket. This point is especially important where subtle shades of colour are required.

(iii) *Scene paints*. These are usually powdered distemper colours, and they are sold in a great range of colours which can be mixed to form such different shades or gradations of colour as you may require. The good and useful basic colours are red, green, blue, yellow, brown, black and whitening.

(iv) *Method for mixing paints*. Half-fill an average-sized bucket with the powder and then add sufficient cold water to create a smooth and fairly thick paste. Stir it with a stick until all is dissolved. No lumps must be left. Then add the solution of pre-prepared size, filling up the bucket.

Size is the binder, and must always be used with scene paint. It does not matter if a hot solution of size is added to the paste, provided the paint is not actually used for working until it has cooled. The paste must thoroughly dissolve and mix with the size.

(v) *Whitening.* Where lighter colours are employed, such as cream or pale blue or pale green, it may be advisable to add whitening to the solution, for this helps to give 'body' or opacity. But remember that the whitening will affect the basic colour, so you should be sure of the result by experimenting beforehand, perhaps on a piece of thick brown paper, and allowing the paint to dry.

If white is to be used as a 'priming' by itself then size must be mixed with it. If, however, the whitening is added to another already prepared colour, then the size in the colour will be sufficient.

Whitening has to be broken up and dissolved in water before mixing it with other colours.

(vi) *Brushes.* The essential requirements are:
(a) A really good 'laying-in' brush (to 'lay in' the basic coat) of 6 in. or 8 in. in width; the softer the better the result in smoothness of surface. The more laying-in brushes you have the better, for then you do not have to keep on washing out the same brush when a different colour is required.

'Laying-in' the basic colour is very important, for it affects of course the general look of the whole design.

(b) Several brushes of different widths, say 4 in. 3 in. and 2 in. They should be flat like the laying-in brushes. These are for more detailed work.

(c) A good selection of lining brushes, from $\frac{1}{2}$ in. to 2 in. in width.

Do not let the brushes stand around in colours. Constantly wash them out. The cleaner the brushes the longer their lives.

Do not forget to have a *straight-edge* available. This is a long flat piece of wood, bevelled on both sides to obtain a straight edge. It is used for marking long lines, such as stripes on wallpaper designs. Also have available a 4-ft rule for marking sizes.

(vii) *Setting up the flats for painting.* They can be fixed against the wall itself, providing that the floor is completely flat and straight. A step-ladder will have to be used for the higher reaches of the flats. Alternatively the flats can be laid on the floor, or supported on trestles. Placing them on the floor is not a particularly comfortable technique, especially if one does not have long-handled brushes.

(viii) *The painting : priming and base coats.* If the flats are new they must be given a priming – a first coat of a solution of size and whitening. This will help to stretch the canvas taut and will provide a working surface for the first colours to be applied to it.

It should be noted that the lining or drawing of details such as panelling or friezes, is done in charcoal *before* the base coat is applied. It is done with charcoal and is then gone over in ink or in indelible pencil, the charcoal being blown or dusted off. The lining will then 'bleed' through or show through the base coat which is painted over it.

The application of the base coat and the intensity of the colour will of course be governed by what the 'base' is supposed to represent. It may be one overall pale colour or a mixture of two or more different colours, thereby giving a variety of tones or a single but subtly graded tone. Remember that in real life colours are not usually simple or unsubtle. A completely white wall, for instance, is never *just* completely white. Look at it and see how the basic colour is affected by light, shadow, age and wear, quite apart from the effect that different times of the day have upon it.

Always try to keep the base coat thin, so as not to overload the canvas with paint.

(ix) *Techniques for giving life to canvas*. There are various techniques that designers use in order to give life to a painted canvas, where a single colour covering an entire area seems too flat or even in tone.

One popular technique is the '*wet blend*' or scumble.

This requires three or more brushes – one for each different colour. These colours are painted on and blended together while they are still wet. The overall effect is of a single colour, but with greater depth of tone. Other methods include:

Sponging. Use a dry sponge and dab the basic coat over all the canvas. Or use a rag-roll. This is literally a rolled-up rag.

Spattering. Rather like action painting; the paint is flicked on.

(x) *Textured surfaces*. These are surfaces which create any kind of realistic, or rough or weathered effect. The most popular form of texturing involves the use of a mixture of whitening and plaster, known as 'spackel'. This is mixed in cold water and then coloured with dye and applied to the surface in thick layers. While it is still damp it can be roughed or grained or 'worked' for greater textural feel. It takes about 24 hours to dry. The flat, or any other piece of scenery, should first be painted in the same colour as the dye used in the spackel.

An alternative method is to mix sawdust and/or wood-chips or shavings with the scene paint and to apply the mixture directly as a texturised coat. A little more size is added to the mixture than is usual with 'straight' scene paint and thus the texture coat is bound more firmly.

(xi) *Stencils*. The setting for many plays involves the use of some kind of domestic interior. The best way to set about the painting of such a set is to think about it in two ways: as a reality, and as a theatricality, and then to see how you can amalgamate the two. For instance, although you may want to represent wallpaper on a stage you will not necessarily use actual wallpaper. This is because wallpaper is much more costly than scene paint, and is difficult to remove if you wish to use the flat again. Also it is sometimes easier to paint the particular design of wallpaper that you want than it is to go out and find as good a design in a shop. A useful device is the stencil. This can be made either from stout brown paper, or from thin show card. After the stencil design has been cut out – and it is best to make two or three copies of the same design as a standby – the whole stencil card is then painted over with knotting. This is a dark brownish liquid, and can be purchased from art shops. This renders the stencil waterproof. If knotting is unobtainable, then quick-drying enamel or gold aluminium paint can be used for the same purpose. In any event, coat the stencil on both sides.

If the stencil is to be used for an all-over design pattern, it is wise, when cutting out the one complete main design, to show a small section of the top and bottom of the two adjacent patterns – this will help the stencilled shapes to fit evenly together.

There are two main ways used to apply the

scene paint through the design of the stencil:

One, is to apply it with a brush as drily as possible, dipping only the tips of the bristles into the paint, and drawing off as much surface paint as can be managed. Otherwise the brush will be too full of paint to obtain a clear impression of the design and the excess paint will run down the canvas after the stencil is removed.

The second method is to use a sponge which has first been dipped into the paint and then squeezed out.

If you use a brush, choose a fairly stiff one, not much more than 2 in. in width, and with bristles $1\frac{1}{2}$ in. or less in length. If you use a sponge, then use one that is easily held in the hand and which is therefore workable. Do not use a big bath sponge.

As a complete alternative, you may use the method known as 'pouncing': first of all the design is pricked out in the stencil sheet with a sharp pin, the pin-holes being very close together. Then the stencil is placed in position over the canvas while a small cotton bag with powdered charcoal in it is dabbed over the design. When the stencil is removed from the canvas the outline is delicately marked, thus enabling the designer to fill in with a brush the different colours as desired. This is, of course, quite a long process.

With any stencilling, first apply the basic colours, then the stencil design, and then work out how to add, say, age, or light and shade.

(xii) *Tapestries*. To create a stage tapestry use the coarsest hessian or clean rough sacking, and paint it with aniline water dyes. The technique with a largish tapestry is to stretch the hessian on a frame so that the colours sink in easily, and so that the stuff is more workable when drawing out the basic design.

Aniline dyes are sold in powder form and can be dissolved in cold water. Or if they are in crystal form they have to be dissolved in hot water. Scene paint can be applied to tapestries, but it is best to use it for judicious blending of the outlines. Scene paint will tend to give the tapestry an overall stiffness, whereas you may want it to hang in soft folds.

Do not use dyes on ordinary canvas flats – that is if you want to use them again at a later date. The dye will always show through any later colour that is used on the flat, no matter how thickly the flat is repainted.

(xiii) *Windows*. These can either be left open, so that the audience can see through to the backing beyond, or they can be opaque and lit from behind by floods or spots carefully placed to give the required effect. (See the design for *Pride and Prejudice* in the next chapter.)

Three materials can be used for 'opaque' windows:

Scenic linen, sometimes called book-linen;

Linen tracing paper;

Ordinary tracing paper. This is of course especially vulnerable to wear and tear.

If you wish to create stained-glass windows, then stretch the opaque linen across the back of the window frame, making sure that it is tightly and evenly stretched and that it is held securely by gluing and tacking. Then draw the outline of your design, lightly in charcoal. If the linen has a shiny surface then make sure it is facing the offstage side of the set. Use aniline water dyes for colour and, if possible, work with a light behind the window so that you can see the effect as you go.

If you want to create an effect of lead, then use very thick black scene paint.

Where a small stained-glass window is

required, for, say, a Victorian hall door or a fanlight, then actual pieces of coloured gelatine (used as filters for stage lights) can be effectively brought into service. It is best to mount these on the back of a design cut out in plywood or thick card.

General points

(a) When painting the basic colours, keep changing the direction of the brush-strokes every three or four strokes. This helps to pull or knit the brush-work together.

(b) Do not forget to paint all edges of flats.

(c) Always mix plenty of size with each bucket of colour.

(d) In marking out any necessary measurements on the flats, such as the layout of panelling, *always* proceed upwards from the base of the flat. Never do the reverse.

(e) Always be prepared to do quite a bit of final painting and touching up when the scenery is actually set up on the stage. Time must be set aside for this when planning the final stages of rehearsal.

(f) The one colour to be very careful of when painting the set is pink. It is so similar to flesh colour that the actors' faces disappear into it.

(g) We have not so far mentioned that useful weapon, the spray gun. This is used to spray on a fine coating of paint where an effect of age, say, or dirt, is required. Some designers will not be seen dead with a spray gun in their hands, while others use it quite liberally. It is not to be used for painting the base coat – for the simple reason that it creates far too fine a coat.

VIII Specific designs

In this chapter we take a look at a small group of very different plays, each of which lends itself readily to school production, and suggest possible approaches to the question of scenic design and staging.

Epic Drama

Illustrations 42 and 43 suggest open-stage designs, suitable for a Greek tragedy or a Shakespeare history. The design creates a simple formality against which the whole action of the play is performed. There need be no stoppages – the action can move from one level to another, or from one area to another without interruption, and any props or items of furniture can be brought on and removed while the play is proceeding.

(i) Such a stage can be set up wherever you wish – in the school hall/church hall, or in a gymnasium, or in the open air.

(ii) Open staging such as this calls for 'open lighting'. This means that all the spotlights are set up on high stands or are connected to convenient beams or rafters in the body of the hall. If the stage area is roughly 20 ft wide and 16 ft deep, then to cover the whole area you will need a minimum of ten spotlights.

All spots should be at least 8 feet from the stage.

(iii) Note that this kind of simple staging creates a wide variety of exits and entrances, quite apart from entrances through the auditorium or entrances created by opening any of the curtains.

(iv) Illustration 43 shows a bird's-eye view of a modified version of illustration 42. It also shows – which would be necessary in both designs – the curtained backing and the all-important 'get-off' steps. In illustration 43 these steps are a part of the overall concept of the design, and are meant to be visible to the audience for certain parts of the play.

(v) Open stages should be constructed in front of or near to any door or doors leading to rooms which the actors can use as dressing-rooms and props-rooms.

(vi) All rostra should be covered in felt and canvas or some form of carpeting.

(vii) The structure must be really secure and well braced.

(viii) The curtains can be hessian or black velvet. If hessian or a lighter cloth is used, then they may need to be backed with some kind of blackout material so that any working light used backstage does not show through.

42   Open stage for epic drama

43 *Bird's-eye view of setting similar to 42, showing
    exit doors for players, and backing*

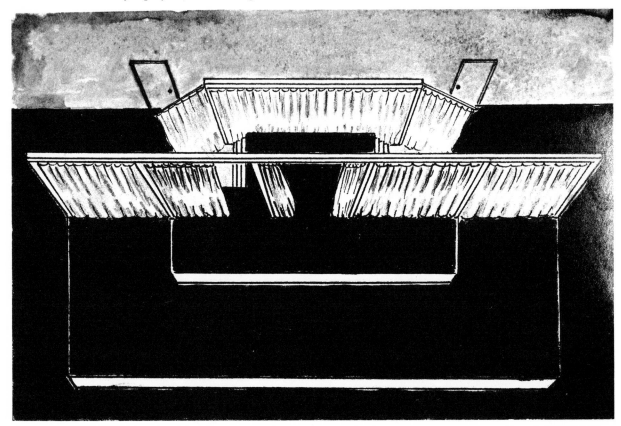

74

Restoration Comedy

The ideas suggested in illustrations 44 and 45, for the staging of a Restoration Comedy, require a stage that is at least 20 ft wide and 14 ft deep. A Molière or a Sheridan play could also be performed against such a setting. The main features of the design are:

Proscenium doors, right and left, opening on to the apron stage;

Large apron;

False proscenium;

Small inner stage, curtained to allow scene changes to be made while the action continues on the main stage and apron.

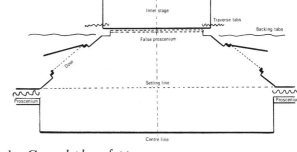

44b   Ground-plan of 44a

44a   Design for Restoration Comedy

Note

1 The proscenium, door pieces, and the false proscenium can be three separate units all cleated together.

2 The inner stage can be raised, but does not have to be.

3 The maskings and backings can be curtains, black or any dark colour.

4 The painted floor is, of course, optional.

5 The proscenium doors can open on stage or offstage, whichever is better.

6 All the decoration and any perspective can be painted. On the other hand, moulding and pilasters can be three dimensional if the designer so wishes.

7 The apron and the downstage should be lit from the f.o.h. The centre stage should be lit from the Number One Spot Bar, and a separate set of spots should be used to light the upstage area behind the false proscenium. A batten with three or four spots could be hung upstage behind the false proscenium and you could also employ cross-lighting from spots in the wings.

45   Working drawing of 44a

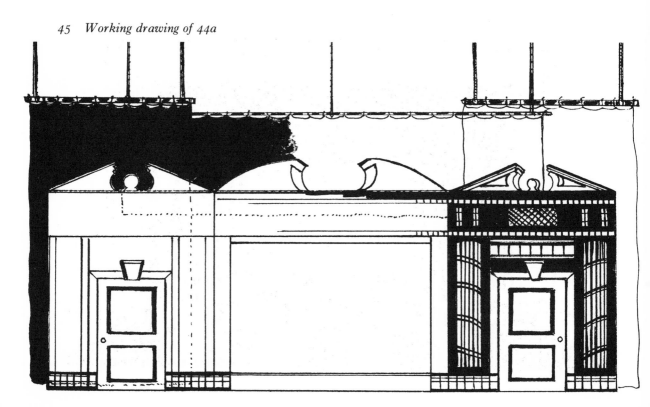

Victorian Music Hall

Illustration 46 shows the way the basic ideas for a Restoration play, in the previous illustrations, can easily be adapted to a useful setting for a Victorian Music Hall or Victorian Melodrama. Indeed the Victorian stage was a development from the Restoration type of stage, with the apron shrunk to a forestage, and the proscenium brought forward.

Instead of doors, this design has two arch flat-pieces set upstage and downstage, with an inner stage above a false proscenium.

46   Adaptation of 44a for Victorian Music Hall/ Melodrama, and showing perspective painting

Macbeth

Illustrations 47a and 47b show the simplest kind of skeletal set for a production of *Macbeth,* in a surround of black curtains and with a cyclorama behind the curtains. Here the angled, scaffold-like broken structure is permanent throughout the action of the play. When the black curtains are opened to reveal the cyclorama, a simple but highly effective contrast is achieved, as shown in the illustrations.

The two main features, then, are:

(a) Skeletal structure.

(b) Cyclorama – to be fully effective this must be adequately lit. This will involve floodlighting from above, and two or three 'troughs' or battens lying along the floor with their light directed upwards at the cyclorama. These battens should be concealed behind a black ground-row, about 18 in. high, running the entire width of the cyclorama. This top and bottom floodlighting should give a good overall spread of light to the cyclorama, and if it is circuited up for three different colour changes, then a good variation of mood can be achieved. Two colour changes will be useful, if three are not possible.

47a *Skeletal set for* Macbeth *in a surround of black curtains with cyclorama behind the curtains*

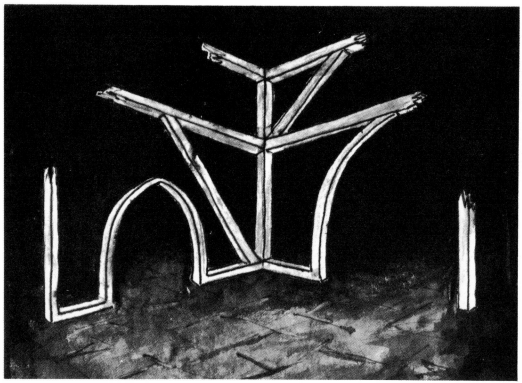

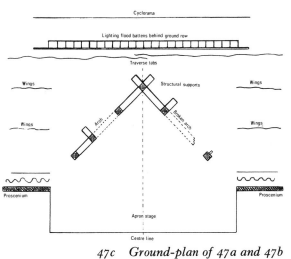

Cyclorama

Lighting flood battens behind ground row

Traverse tabs

Wings

Wings

Structural supports

Arch

Broken arch

Wings

Wings

Proscenium

Proscenium

Apron stage

Centre line

47c Ground-plan of 47a and 47b

47b Showing the cyclorama

Note

1 To light a cyclorama effectively, there must be reasonable depth to a stage. Otherwise, the lights directed at the downstage and centre-stage areas will spill over on to the cyclorama, and the actors' shadows will be thrown on to the cyclorama. Ideally, the ground-row battens should be at least 3 or 4 feet in front of the cyclorama.

2 If the stage is fairly small, then this is an additional argument for building some kind of apron in front of it, perhaps at a different level or group of levels. It is virtually impossible to achieve really interesting atmosphere on a stage which suggests lack of space, especially where a large cast has to be moved about in a convincing and impressive style.

3 Black surrounds are essential, in order that stark contrasts can be achieved, and that much can be lost into the darkness.

Pride and Prejudice

Illustrations 48a–d show a simple unit setting for *Pride and Prejudice*. This has been chosen because the most popular adaptation of the novel requires three different interior sets, thereby creating the basic problem – how to ring the changes within the limitations of the average school stage and wing space? The design illustrated here solves the problem with a stylised permanent setting made up with screens, and with three different and interchangeable central window units.

    48a represents the Bennetts' house

    48b represents the Aunt's house

    48c represents the country home of Lady Catherine.

The chief technical problem is the construction of the three interchanging window units. They must all three be constructed separately on trucks so that each one can be moved into position while the other two are stored offstage.

Note

1 If the actual windows are opaque, then there will need to be no view through the windows – i.e. no backings.

2 If the stage is surrounded by black curtains – or any other colour – they will provide sufficient masking, even if the doors are required to open on to the stage. In the illustrations, the doors open off the stage.

48   *Screen setting for* Pride and Prejudice

a   *Act I*

3 The fireplace piece is the same in both the sets, but it is in two different positions. There is no need in this type of stylised setting to disguise it. Only a change of ornaments is necessary.

4 There is no reason why the flats should not be perfectly straight pieces if desired. The screen-like decorative shape is purely optional.

5 The window opening only needs to be 6 feet at the most.

6 Use a minimum amount of furniture.

7 The setting must be securely braced and supported.

8 When the window pieces are in position they should be securely attached to the permanent standing flats. Then all the units will give support to each other.

9 The offstage sides of the screens must be well masked by curtains.

10 Keep all the main lighting on the acting area. But this does not prevent the use of some kind of back lighting, i.e. light directed on to the opaque windows. But you must be careful to see that no back lighting spills over the top of the set. If, for example, the light is provided by a couple of floods on stands, make sure that the spread of light is directed on to the actual area of the window. If the spread is too great then mask down the front of the floods with cardboard.

b Act II

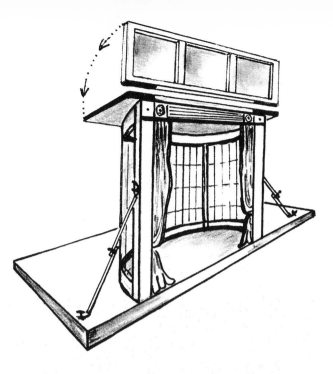

*d   Example of window unit in a and independent
     fireplace unit in a and b*

c   Act III

Gaslight

Illustrations 49 and 50 show a box-setting for *Gaslight*. This has been chosen to illustrate what is basically a simple and easy shape – as the bird's-eye view in 50 shows – and to illustrate the way this simple concept can be elaborated with fittings and furnishings into something most effective. This same idea can be adapted into a number of very different 'atmospheres': Shaw's *Candida* for instance,

or Wilde's *The Importance of Being Earnest*. It can also be fashioned into a setting for an Ibsen play or a Chekhov. It may well be that the substitution of, say, a stove for a fireplace, becomes the central feature round which the new design is moulded.

Note

1 The aim of this kind of setting is to re-create an interior with as much reality as possible, so that the audience while looking at what seems to be a three-dimensional photograph are drawn into and involved in the drama.

49 *Box-setting for* Gaslight

2 This set can be adapted quite easily to differently sized stages. If, for instance, the stage is a very small one, then the fireplace also will be very small. Or it can be enlarged into something very ornate and elaborate for a much bigger stage.

3 If the design involves the use of a ceiling-piece, this will have to be hung first and then kept out of the way while the walls of the set are put in position. There must be anchorage to which the three ropes supporting the ceiling can be securely tied. Otherwise dispense altogether with the idea of a ceiling and just 'lose' the top part of the set into the black borders. If, however, a ceiling is possible, remember always that the edge nearest the audience is hardly ever flush with the downstage edge of the setting-line; it is usually set at least 4 feet upstage. If this is not done, then the lighting from the Number One Spot Bar is obstructed by the ceiling.

Any kind of central hanging lamp or chandelier is usually suspended from a rope of its own and hung immediately in front of the downstage edge of the ceiling-piece. It is not usually hung through a hole in the ceiling, for this ruins an otherwise good canvas flat which cannot then be used again.

50 Showing the basic simplicity of 49

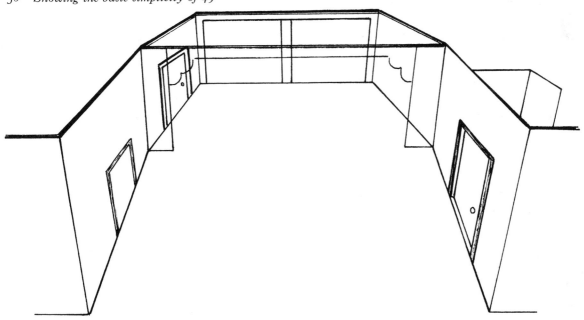

Postscript

Finally, it may be useful to summarise some of the general points we have made:

1 Choose a play/show which is right for the school, its background, its drama traditions, and the personalities of its pupils.

2 For your first venture into direction or designing, do not choose a vast project. Begin with that which is technically the simplest.

3 Study the defects and limitations of your stage and hall and experiment with all the various ways of overcoming them.

4 Do not, in your production, have everything done *for* the pupils: involve them actively in every stage of the operation. Give a talented pupil the opportunity to design or direct the play himself.

5 Plan the production in detail.

6 In every aspect of the work involved – experiment.

7 With costumes – make sure that every actor feels confident in whatever he wears on stage.

8 With lighting – light the actors, not their feet, and not the scenery.

9 In designing the sets, make sure that they will work easily on the particular stage where they are to be used. Similarly, think always of the shape and colours of the sets as they will actually be seen on the stage. What looks fine as a small sketch may look grotesque when blown up to the dimensions of the stage.

Terms used in staging and scenic design

Acting areas These represent the whole area of the stage that is visible to the audience. This is divided up as in illustration 25.

Apron stage Any kind of addition to the stage, whether permanent or temporary, built in front of the proscenium. It can be of the same height as the main stage, but it does not have to be. Nor does it have to be all of one level, nor does it have to be uniform in shape.

Backcloth A large, high and wide canvas with wooden battens at the top and base.

Backing A piece of scenery placed behind another piece to give some kind of realistic backing: for example, a view of a street placed behind a hall window. See illustration 8.

Back wall This refers to the back wall of the stage, not of the auditorium.

Batten A length of wood.

Blacks A set of black curtains suspended in the wings, across the back of the stage and across the top of the stage (borders) – thus surrounding and enclosing the acting areas of the stage.

Boat truck A low platform on wheels or castors, on which heavy pieces such as thrones or pillars can be built and which can therefore be easily moved. Usually the wheels are hidden as much as possible by a masking surround of wood, like a box lid. This must not be completely flush with the floor or else the truck will scrape the floor when it is moved.

Book flat Two flats of any size or shape, hinged together which when opened like a book at an angle of say 45 degrees, will be self-supporting.

Borders Long strips of canvas or cloth hanging one behind the other and stretching from stage left to stage right. Used to conceal from the view of the audience anything above the *top* of the scenery. The usual number on the average stage is three. See illustration 12a.

Box-set A stage design in which the two sides and the back of the stage are hidden behind a combination of flats, the flats representing, for example, three walls of a room. See illustrations 19 and 20.

Brace A wooden or iron support attached to the back of a flat. The brace is hooked into a screw-eye fixed to the batten of a flat, and the other end is screwed down to the stage floor at an angle. The wooden brace is adjustable and can be lengthened or shortened while the iron brace cannot. If it is not permitted to screw into the stage floor, then the base end of the brace must be secured by weights. As braces stand out from the flat which they are supporting, at an angle of about 45 degrees, then consideration must be given beforehand to the problem of the amount of space that they will take up.

There is also the *french brace*. This is attached permanently to a self-supporting unit of scenery by means of screwed-on hinges. This enables the brace to act as a flap and to be folded back when not in use. It also enables speedy setting up of scenery and speedy removal. See illustrations 39a–f.

Ceiling-piece A 'flat' or a piece of stretched canvas attached to a wooden frame, hung by ropes and then lowered into position so that it rests on top of the box-set flats and forms a roof or ceiling. It is always made large enough to extend beyond the edges of the flats, both at sides and back by about 2 ft.

Cleat A metal or wooden hook fixed about 18 in. from the top of a flat on the back of the right-hand stile.

Cleat line A thin rope fixed about 18 in. from the top of a flat on the back of the left-hand stile.

Cleating The method of joining one flat to another. The left-hand line of flat number 1 is thrown over the right-hand cleat hook of flat number 2. The line is then pulled tightly down (either straight or zigzagged) and then tied up at the base. See illustration 26.

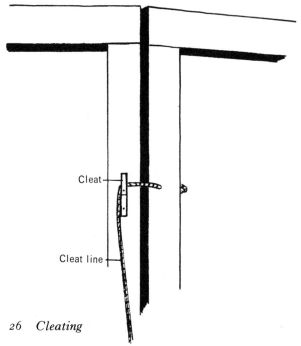

Cleat

Cleat line

26 *Cleating*

Composite sets There are two kinds:
1 Several different localities are incorporated into one design, perhaps with each locality on a different level. The action of the play moves from one place to another without any kind of

interruption. This kind of setting is needed, for instance, in *A View from the Bridge* or *Stephen D.*

2 A single, highly stylised setting in which changes of location are marked simply by changes of lighting or by bringing on small units of scenery/furniture.

Counter-weight Round iron weight, about 4 in. thick, with a portion cut out. Used to weigh down braces if they cannot otherwise be secured. See illustration 39.

Cut cloth Same as a backcloth, but with some section cut out, usually the centre, in whatever shape is required.

Cut-out flat A flat in which the top and sides are cut to show the actual profile and shape of the object it is supposed to represent – for example, a church steeple, or the gable of a house. Also known as a profile flat.

Cyclorama Often known simply as the 'cyc'. A large high and wide backcloth, tightly stretched across the back of the acting area of the stage to represent sky or space. It is either white or pale blue. It is never painted. Sometimes, when it is smooth enough, the back wall of the stage can be used as the cyc.

Dock The area backstage used for storing scenery.

Downstage That part of the acting area of the stage which is nearest to the audience. See 'acting areas'.

Edges The very important *thickness* of the flat which is sometimes forgotten about in painting. If the flat is angled at all then some of the edges are of course visible to the audience and must be properly painted.

Elevation A drawing, on the same scale as the ground-plan, of the units employed in the design.

False proscenium A temporary arch set upstage of the permanent proscenium, and usually smaller in width and height than the permanent one.

Flat A unit of scenery made of canvas stretched out on a wooden frame.

Flies The space above the scenery or setting, where scenery can be hung or 'flown' while not in use.

Floats Usually called footlights. They are placed in the floor immediately in front of the main curtains. The word 'floats' derives from the days when, before gas and electricity, the footlights were lamps of wick floating in oil.

Floodlights See chapter V.

Front cloth Movable cloth, hung across the front of the stage.

Front-of-house The auditorium.

Front-of-house spots Spotlights fixed or standing in the front-of-house. Not to be confused with house lights.

Front-of-house tabs Main proscenium curtain.

Gels Shortened word for 'gelatine', the substance from which colour filters are made for placing in front of spotlights. Also called 'jellies'.

Ground-plan Scaled drawing of the set as viewed from above.

Ground-row A low piece of independent scenery, often placed a few feet downstage of a backcloth or cyclorama, and perhaps used to hide from the audience's view any lighting battens used to illuminate the backcloth or cyclorama.

House lights Lights which light up the auditorium before and after the show, and during the interval.

Inset A small setting, inside another one, used for example in a prologue, and then removed.

Lighting batten A length of wood or steel rod to which are affixed lights.

Lines Ropes.

Masking-piece Anything that completely blocks out anything that the audience should not see.

Offstage Any part of the stage that is unseen by the audience.

O.P. Short for 'opposite prompt'. Traditionally the prompter sits stage left, and hence O.P. refers to the right-hand side, i.e. the actor's right when facing the audience.

Pin-hinge A hinge whose two pieces are pivoted together by a pin.

Profile flat See cut-out flat.

P.S. Prompt side.

Props Any portable items/properties brought on or taken off during the course of the play. Props table – where the smaller props are kept; usually in the wings stage left.

Proscenium Roman term for the area on which the actors actually performed. Nowadays we use the term chiefly to refer to the proscenium arch, which is the main arch at the front of the stage, separating the stage from the auditorium.

Rails Horizontal framework of a flat.

Raked stage A stage sloping upwards from the proscenium arch to the back wall.

Ramp A raked rostrum of any size or shape.

Returns The two black flats which flank both sides of the set, and are placed about 2 ft from the proscenium arch and run offstage parallel with the proscenium arch. They mark the sides of the downstage edge of the sets. They are the first two flats to be fixed into position when erecting the set. And if, for instance, the proscenium opening is 22 ft and the designer has produced a setting which is 21 ft wide, then the returns, instead of their edges being flush with the width of the proscenium arch, will have to be set 6 in. on stage. The returns are clearly shown on illustrations 8 and 20.

Reveal Unit added to the flat of a door or arch to give an appearance of solidity. See illustration 37.

Set-up The actual setting up of the scenery on the stage.

Setting-line Line drawn on the ground-plan from the P.S. return to the O.P. return and marking the 'fourth wall' of the set: i.e. showing the line beyond which no scenery is set downstage.

Sight lines The lines marking off the maximum and minimum areas of the stage visible to the audience.

Sill All doors and arches have an iron sill which runs along the floor to give strength and support between the two uprights.

Size Glue in powder or jelly form. Powder has to be stirred into boiling water. Jelly needs to be liquefied in a bucket over a flame. 1 lb of powdered size is required per bucket of water. All distemper powder paints must be mixed with size, or they will rub or flake off when they are dry.

Spray gun Employed to spray a fine coat of paint on to scenery.

Stage cloth A tough canvas floor cloth, covering the main part of the stage, and usually extending in width and depth to the actual setting surrounding the acting area. It can be painted with scene paint, or aniline dyes can be used. If the stage floor is visible to parts or all of the audience, then the painting of the floor should be an intrinsic part of the scenic design.

Standing set A set which remains unchanged throughout the play.

Stiles The vertical wooden framework of a flat.

Tabs Curtains.

Traverse tabs Curtains hanging upstage of the main curtains, and which can be closed to con-

ceal the upstage area, perhaps while scenery is being changed.

Trucks Any kind of movable unit built on castors and which can easily be moved around the stage. Flats or double-sided flats can be placed on the trucks, and so can three-dimensional units.

Unit set Settings in which main features of the scenery remain throughout the play, and to which are added various units to indicate changes of scene.

Vision scene A device in which gauze is fixed and tightly stretched over an opening and then painted so that it looks solid when lit up from the front, but which becomes transparent when lit up from behind – thus achieving a 'vision' effect.

Vista scene A standard scenic idea of the eighteenth and nineteenth centuries. Receding wing-pieces were erected, one behind the other and on both sides of the stage. The space on stage centre, between the pairs of pieces, decreased the farther away one got from the proscenium, thus creating an illusion of vista/distance.

Index

Acting areas 87
Angled open stage 18
Apron stage 13, 15, 16, 76, 80, 87
Arena stage – see open stage and theatre in
    the round
Assistant stage managers 20

Baby spot 44
Back wall 87
Backcloth 33, 87
Backings 50, 51, 87
Backstage 15
Battens 50, 87, 89
Bird's eye view perspectives 27
Blacks 87
Boat truck 87
Book flat 59, 66, 87
Borders 87
Box set 36, 84, 88
Bracing 61, 82, 88
Brushes 68
Butt end joint 56

Candida 84

Canvas 58, 64, 68
Carpenter 20
Castors 65
Catering 20
Ceiling-piece 85, 88
Chandelier 85
Chekhov 84
Cleat line 88
Cleating 88
Colour filters 51, 67
Composite sets 24, 88
Costumes 17, 23, 30 *et seq*, 86
Cotton 31
Counter-weight 89
Curtain sets 33
Curtains 43
Cut cloth 89
Cyclorama 40, 41, 78, 89
    lighting the cyclorama, 50, 80

Designer
    basic kinds of design 33 *et seq*
    elevation 27
    examples of specific sets 72 *et seq*

general principles 12, 86
ground-plan 25
ideas to paper 24 *et seq*
model 28
sight lines 29
Director
arena staging 17
director and designer 24 *et seq*
general principles 12, 20, 21, 23, 86
Dock 89
Doors 59
Downstage 89
Dress rehearsals 23
Dressing rooms 15
Dyes 70

Edges 89
Electrician 15, 20, 54
Elevation 27, 89

Flats 28, 29, 36, 56 *et seq*, 81, 89
book flats 59, 66
cut-out flats 41, 89
edges of, 89
painting 68
window, door and fireplace flats 59, 82
Fireplaces 59, 82
Flexible staging 13
Floats 89
Floor of stage 17, 42, 76
Floodlights 43, 45 *et seq*, 89
Focus lantern 44
Fresnel spot 44
Friezes 68
Front cloth 89
Front-of-house 20, 89
Front-of-house spots 10, 89
Front-of-house tabs 89

Gangways 16

Gaslight 84
Gels 89
Glue 58
Greek tragedy 72
Grooving 66
Ground-plan of lighting 52
of sets 25, 89
Ground row 66, 89
Gymnasium 15, 72

Halls 13, 15
Halved joint 56
Handbills 31
Hessian 31, 70, 73
House lights 90

Ibsen 84
Importance of Being Earnest 84
Improvisation 11, 21
Inset 90
Inset stage 76

Joints 56

Knotting 69

Lighting
approach to lighting 46 *et seq*
basic principles 42, 86
colour filters 51
designer 30, 42 *et seq*, 51
directional lighting 43
front-of-house lights 55
ground-plan 52
house lights 90
lighting battens 90
lighting cues 54
lighting director 54
mood and atmosphere 51
open lighting 72

setting up 23, 54
Lines 90

Macbeth 78 *et seq*
Masking-piece 90
Melodrama 77
Merchant of Venice 24
Mirror-profile spot 44
Model 28
Molière 75
Mortice and tenon joint 56, 58
Music Director 20
Music Hall 21, 51, 77
Musicals 11, 23

Number One Spot Bar 46 *et seq*, 76
Number Two Spot Bar 50
Nylon 31

Offstage 90
O.P. 90

Painting 67 *et seq*, 71
Pin-hinge 90
Pouncing 70
Production Conference 21
Production Manager 20, 21, 22, 32
Production schedule 22
Profile scenery 66, 90
Programmes 23, 31, 32
Project 21
Prompter 15
Props 17, 90
Proscenium 28, 90
  false proscenium 59, 76, 77, 89

Rails 56, 90
Raked stage 90
Ramp 90
Rehearsal schedule 20, 22, 23

Restoration Comedy 63, 75, 77
Returns 90
Reveal 90
Revue 11, 57
Ropes 61
Rostra 11, 62, 63 *et seq*, 73

Satin 31
Screens 11, 82
Seating 16, 17
Setting-line 90
Shakespeare 72, 78
Sheridan 75
Sight lines 29, 90
Silk 31
Sill 90
Size 67, 68, 90
Sound and effects 15, 20, 23
Space 15
Spattering 69
Sponging 69
Spotlights 43 *et seq*
Spray gun 71, 91
Stage
  angled open stage 18
  apron 13, 15, 16, 76, 80, 87
  bare 33
  independant 33
  open 11, 16, 42, 72
  raked 90
Stage cloth 91
Stage Director or Stage Manager 20, 30
Stained glass 70, 71
Staircase 62 *et seq*
Stencils 69
Stephen D 20
Steps 62 *et seq*, 73
Stiles 56, 91

Tabs 91

Tacking 58, 66
Tapestries 70
Textured surfaces 69
Theatre in the round 11, 16
Traverse tabs 91
Truck units 41, 65, 91

Unit set 91

View from the Bridge 89
Vision scene 91

Vista scene 91

Wallpaper 69
Wardrobe 20, 22, 30 *et seq*, 86
Wet blend 69
Whitening 68
Windows 59, 70, 81
Wings 16
  cut-out wings 33
Wool 31